MYTHOLOGY OF INDIA

MYTHS AND LEGENDS OF INDIA, TIBET AND SRI LANKA

RACHEL STORM

southwater

This edition is published by Southwater

Southwater is an imprint of Anness Publishing Ltd
Hermes House, 88–89 Blackfriars Road, London SE1 8HA
tel. 020 7401 2077; fax 020 7633 9499
www.southwaterbooks.com; info@anness.com

© Anness Publishing Ltd 2000, 2003

This edition distributed in the UK by The Manning Partnership Ltd,
6 The Old Dairy, Melcombe Road, Bath BA2 3LR;
tel. 01225 478 444; fax 01225 478 440; sales@manning-partnership.co.uk

This edition distributed in the USA and Canada by National Book Network,
4720 Boston Way, Lanham, MD 20706;
tel. 301 459 3366; fax 301 459 1705; www.nbnbooks.com

This edition distributed in Australia by Pan Macmillan Australia,
Level 18, St Martins Tower, 31 Market St, Sydney, NSW 2000;
tel. 1300 135 113; fax 1300 135 103; customer.service@macmillan.com.au

This edition distributed in New Zealand by The Five Mile Press (NZ) Ltd,
PO Box 33–1071 Takapuna, Unit 11/101–111 Diana Drive, Glenfield, Auckland 10;
tel. (09) 444 4144; fax (09) 444 4518; fivemilenz@clear.net.nz

A CIP catalogue record for this book is available from the British Library.

Publisher: Joanna Lorenz
Managing Editor: Helen Sudell
Project Editor: Emma Gray
Contributing Editor: Beverley Jollands
Designer: Mario Bettella, Artmedia
Map Illustrator: Stephen Sweet
Picture Researcher: Adrian Bentley
Editorial Reader: Richard McGinlay
Production: Don Campaniello

1 3 5 7 9 10 8 6 4 2

Previously published as part of a larger compendium, *Myths of the East*

Page 1: Avalokiteshvara, the bodhisattva of universal compassion.
Page 2: Lakshmi, consort of Viruna.
Page 3: Maitreya, the buddha of the future, and the last earthly buddha.
Page 4: The god Krishna.
Page 5: Tara, in her white form, the symbol of transcendent knowledge.

Publisher's Note
The entries in this book are all listed alphabetically. Where more than one name
exists for a character the entry is listed under the name used in the original
country of origin for that particular myth. Names in italic capital letters indicate
that that name has an individual entry. Special feature spreads examine specific
mythological themes more fully. If a character is included in a special feature
spread it is noted at the end of their individual entry.

MYTHOLOGY OF
INDIA

CONTENTS

INTRODUCTION

THE IMMENSE INDIAN subcontinent encompasses an astonishing diversity of geographical regions. In the north lie the rugged Himalayan mountains, further south the vast agricultural plains of the river Ganges; there are high plateaux and low-lying coastal regions, vast rainforests and deserts. The climate is extreme, with scorching heat followed by drenching monsoons. This tremendously varied and unpredictable land has given rise to a rich mythology, many of whose deities have spread elsewhere, for example to Tibet and Sri Lanka, the other countries that are under consideration here.

A significant feature of Indian belief is the desire to transcend the chaos and unpredictability of the world in order to find the truth, nirvana (spiritual ecstasy) or enlightenment. From the earliest times, evidence suggests that people believed that they might achieve this goal through the practice of meditation. For example, modern excavations have uncovered evidence that the people of the Indus Valley civilization, which flourished around the middle of the third millennium BC in the region of modern Pakistan, worshipped a deity associated with meditation.

In the second millennium BC, the remarkable Indus Valley civilization collapsed under the constant incursions of the Aryan invaders, a group of Bronze Age tribes. The Aryans, or

GAUTAMA BUDDHA, the founder of Buddhism, attained enlightenment after many incarnations as a bodhisattva, or "buddha-to-be", setting an example for all Buddhists to follow. (GANDHARA-STYLE RELIEF, 3RD CENTURY BC.)

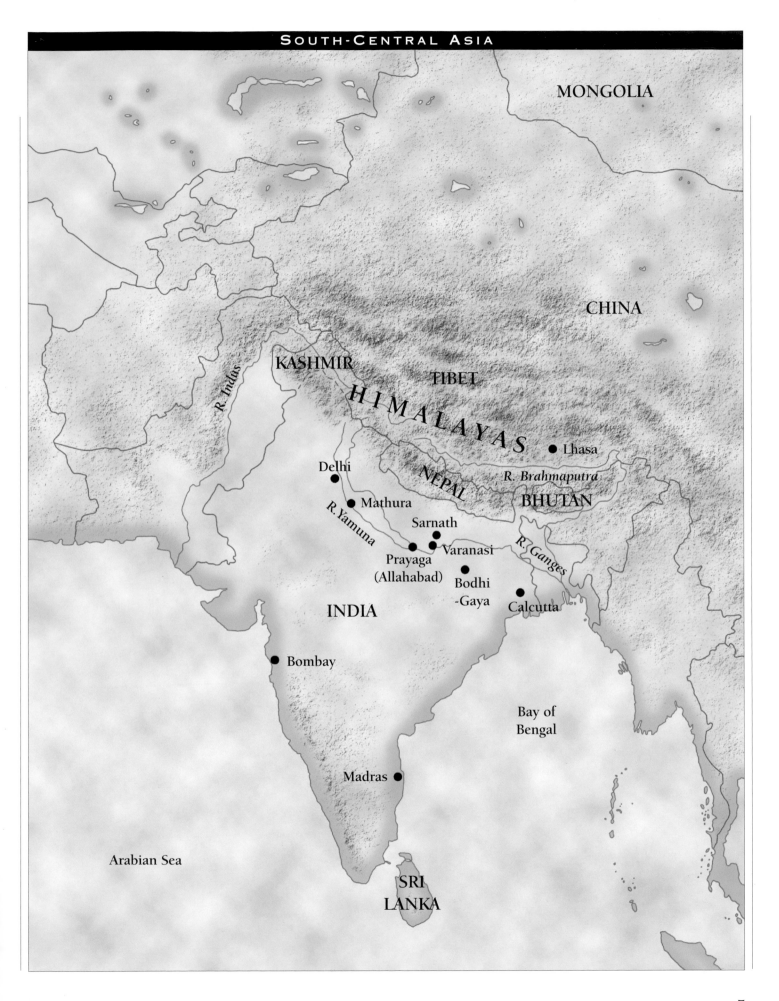

SOUTH-CENTRAL ASIA

MONGOLIA

CHINA

KASHMIR

TIBET

HIMALAYAS

R. Indus

Lhasa

Delhi

NEPAL

R. Brahmaputra

R. Yamuna

Mathura

BHUTAN

Sarnath

Varanasi

R. Ganges

Prayaga
(Allahabad)

Bodhi
-Gaya

Calcutta

INDIA

Bombay

Bay of
Bengal

Madras

Arabian Sea

SRI
LANKA

"Noble Folk", believed in many gods, spirits and demons. Among their most important deities were Indra, a weather and warrior god; Varuna, a maintainer of order and morality; Agni, a fire god; Surya, a sun god; and Yama, king of the dead.

Many of the gods of the Aryan invaders are venerated in India to this day. None the less, some of the beliefs attributed to the people of the Indus Valley civilization were to resurface. For example, the great Hindu god Shiva is believed to have taken on some of the characteristics of the Indus Valley civilization's fertility god. Indeed, this ancient figure is sometimes known as "proto-Shiva". The god also demonstrates something of the continuity of Indian belief, the willingness of the people to adopt and assimilate deities into their own world-view. In the *Rig Veda*, a

collection of sacred hymns composed between the 14th and tenth centuries BC, Shiva is only a minor deity known as Rudra. However, he later rose to become one of the three major gods of Hinduism, the belief system that developed from India's earlier religious traditions and prevails. Shiva also embodies the implicit contradictions of Hindu belief: that genesis cannot take place without previous destruction and that the ordered cosmos can only evolve from an initial state of chaos. Thus, though Shiva is known as the "Destroyer", his name means "Auspicious"; he is an ascetic (denying physical pleasures), but he is also extremely wild and has a huge sexual appetite.

Whereas the Aryans believed that after death they would either ascend to the heavens or descend to the underworld, by the

MANDALAS symbolize the universe as a circle. Though often found in paintings, for ritual purposes they are drawn in rice or coloured powder on consecrated ground. The dance called mandala-nrtya, performed in a circle, is based on Krishna's dance with the gopis and symbolizes the constant presence of the god. (DETAIL OF MANDALA OF BODHISATTVA AMOGHAPASA, GOUACHE, NEPAL, 1860.)

time of the *Upanishads*, sacred teachings composed between the eighth and fifth centuries BC, the human condition had come to be seen as one in which people were trapped within a relentless cycle of birth and death. The goal was to transcend the cycle and achieve liberation. It may be that such ideas, totally absent from the teachings of the Aryan invaders, had their roots in the beliefs of the Indus Valley civilization.

Followers of Buddhism and Jainism, two religions which arose in India in the sixth century BC, were also dedicated to the use of

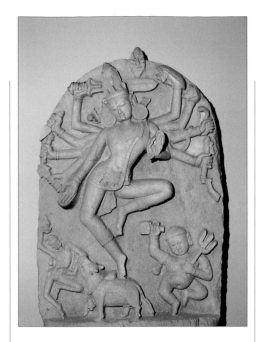

SHIVA as Nataraja, "Lord of the Dance", represents creation and destruction in balance. He is supported by the bull, Nandi. (STONE CARVING, 12-13TH CENTURY.)

meditative techniques as a means of release from the cycle of death and rebirth. For Jains, the path to liberation demanded that stringent austerities, including self-mortifications, be practised, while Buddhists emphasized the inward struggle. Although both Buddhism and Jainism deny the existence of a creator god, they have a rich mythology. Jainism focuses on the tirthankaras, the great teachers who show the way to achieve liberation. Buddhism, on the other hand, gave rise to the cult of buddhas and bodhisattvas ("buddhas-to-be"), who helped people along the path to enlightenment.

Veneration of the numerous buddhas and bodhisattvas smoothed the way for the assimilation of Buddhism by people used to deity worship. Moreover, the adoption of many deities from Hinduism, as well as other religions, helped Buddhism to spread and flourish. At the same time, such a policy produced a vast and often bewildering pantheon.

In the third century BC, Mahinda, a close relative of the great Indian emperor Ashoka, introduced Buddhism to Sri Lanka. The king of Sri Lanka was converted, and Buddhism became the country's dominant religion, remaining so to this day. In the seventh century AD, Buddhist missionaries travelled from

VISHNU was seen as the protector of the world. His first incarnation, or avatar, was as the fish, Matsya. (WOODCUT BY BERNARD PICART, 18TH CENTURY.)

India to Tibet. Although the new beliefs faced resistance from followers of the indigenous Bon religion, by the 12th century, Buddhism was firmly entrenched.

The Bon religion was characterized by a belief in the existence of two creator deities, the principles of good and evil, as well as a host of lesser gods and goddesses, and shared some similarities with shamanism. Buddhist teachers adopted many of the old shamanistic rites, attempting to contact the spirit world, and would often take the role of oracles or divine soothsayers for those Bon deities that had been brought into the new religion. This assimilation produced a very individual form of Buddhism, sometimes known as Lamaism,

from the title, "Lama", given to Tibetan Buddhist religious masters or gurus. In time, Lamaism spread to Nepal, Mongolia and Bhutan.

Within India, Buddhism was largely reabsorbed into Hinduism; the Buddha himself was said to have come into being as the ninth incarnation of the great Hindu god Vishnu. This continual absorption and assimilation of different beliefs is perhaps the dominant characteristic of Indian religion. Certainly, it is what has helped give rise to such a rich and varied mythology.

THE MYTHS AND LEGENDS

A

THE ADIBUDDHA, or "Primordial Buddha", rose to prominence in the 11th century as a result of an attempt to transform Mahayana, or "Great Vehicle" Buddhism, into a monotheistic religion, inspired by a sentence within a Buddhist text, which claimed that there was a self-emanating buddha who existed long before anything else. In Nepal, the Adibuddha came to be seen as infinite, omniscient and the supreme creator. It was said that he emanated from the mystic syllable "Om" and gave rise to the five *DHYANIBUDDHAS*, or "Great Buddhas of Wisdom".

In Tantric Buddhism, Vajradhara is identified with the Adibuddha, and is portrayed holding a bell and a thunderbolt. In Nepal and Tibet, the Adibuddha is usually shown wearing robes and the ornaments of a *BODHISATTVA*. His *SHAKTI*, or female energy, is Adidharma.

THE ADIBUDDHA or "Primordial Buddha", in the posture of Yab-Yum ("Father-Mother") with his shakti. (BRASS AND COPPER, TIBET, 16TH CENTURY.)

ADITI, a Hindu mother goddess, is regarded as the personification of the earth, and her bosom as its navel. Her name means "Infinity" or "Free from Bounds". She is symbolized by the immortal cow and is said to embody unlimited light, consciousness and unity.

Aditi is usually said to be the mother of the great god *VISHNU*, and she appears in the Veda, the "sacred knowledge" of the Hindus, as the consort of *BRAHMA* or *KASYAPA. DAKSHA*, the son of Brahma, is said to have been born of Aditi, and Aditi to have been born of him. The goddess is also the mother of the *ADITYAS*, the deities who protect the world from chaos and ignorance. She rules over

the divine ordering of the world and is said to be able to free all those who believe in her from sickness and sin. Whereas Aditi corresponds to the universal and divine in humankind, her sister, Diti, corresponds to all that is individual, human and divided.

THE ADITYAS are the offspring of *ADITI*, the Hindu mother goddess. They are usually said to number seven or eight deities, including *MITRA* and *VARUNA*. However, in later times, there were sometimes said to be 12 Adityas, each of whom was associated with the sun as the source of life, and each connected with a month of the year.

The Adityas are believed to offer salvation from all ills. Martanda, the eighth son of Aditi, is sometimes regarded as the divine ancestor of human beings.

THE ADIBUDDHA, in Tibetan Buddhism, is the personification of pure sunyata, or emptiness, combined with wisdom. All buddhas are aspects of his nature. (TIBETAN PAINTING.)

AGASTYA was a great Hindu sage who was said to have been conceived when the beautiful Urvasi, one of the *APSARAS*, slept with both *MITRA* (or sometimes *SURYA*) and *VARUNA*. Agastya caused any obstacle that stood in the way of the well-being of the universe to disappear. When a range of mountains threatened to grow so high that it hid the light of the sun, Agastya begged it to shrink back down in order to let him pass, and to stay that size until he returned. The sage then tricked the mountain range by returning home along another route. On another occasion, Agastya helped the hero *RAMA*, an *AVATAR* of the great god *VISHNU*. When Rama went into battle against *RAVANA*, the king of *LANKA*, he shot off each of the demon's ten heads with his arrows. However, the hero found that as soon as one head was removed, another sprang up in its place. Rama finally produced a miraculous weapon which had been given to him by Agastya. The weapon's point was made of sunlight and fire, and it weighed as much as the mountains *MERU* and

AGNI (left) spouts flames and carries a
torch or flaming spear. (FRENCH, 19TH CENTURY.)

AGNI (right), as the god of sacrificial fire,
is a mediator between gods and
humankind. (BRONZE, ORISSA, 11-12TH CENTURY.)

Mandara put together. The arrow
struck Ravana, killed him, and then
magically returned to Rama.

AGNI, or "Fire", is one of the
chief deities of the *Rig Veda*, the
sacred hymns of Hinduism. He is
both the protective god of the
hearth and the god of the sacrificial
fire. In the latter role, he mediates
between deities and human beings
by taking sacrifices to the gods.
Agni appears in the sky as lightning
and is regarded as both cruel and
kind: although he dispels darkness,
he devoured his parents as soon as
he was born and consumes the
bodies on the cremation pyre. He
is referred to as the son of heaven
and earth, and is usually said to
have emerged either from the sun
or from lightning. Other sources

regard him as the son of *ADITI* and
KASYAPA, and he is sometimes said
to have been born from stone or
from the rubbing together of two
pieces of wood.

One of the guardian deities of
the world, Agni can grant immortality and purify people of their sins
after death. He looked after the
monkey god *HANUMAN* when the
demon king of *LANKA*, *RAVANA*, set
light to his tail. The god is portrayed as red in colour, with two or
three heads, several arms, a long
beard and clothes of flames. He is

*AIRAVATA, the great white elephant,
carries Indra into combat with Krishna,
who is mounted on Garuda. Krishna was to
overcome Indra. (WATERCOLOUR, C. 1590.)*

sometimes shown riding in a chariot drawn by horses but is also said
to ride a ram or a goat.

AIRAVATA, according to Hindu
mythology, was the great white elephant ridden by *INDRA*, the king of
the gods. One myth tells how the
goddess *PARVATI* invited all the gods
to a great party held to celebrate the
birth of her son, *GANESHA*. Sani, the
planet Saturn, at first refused the
invitation, but Parvati insisted that
he accept. When Sani looked at
Ganesha, the child's head was
reduced to ashes. *VISHNU*, the preserver of the universe, went in
search of another head for
Ganesha, and returned with that of
the elephant Airavata.

AKSOBHYA, one of the five *DHYANIBUDDHAS*, or "Great Buddhas of Wisdom", rules over the eastern paradise Abhirati. His name means "Immovable", and he is said to subjugate the passions and enjoy mirror-like wisdom. Long ago, when Aksobhya was a monk, he vowed before the buddha who then ruled over Abhirati that he would never experience anger or repulsion. After endlessly striving to achieve this goal, he finally became a buddha and took up rulership over Abhirati. Anyone who is reborn in Abhirati will never fall into lower levels of consciousness, so all believers seek, like Aksobhya, to conquer passion.

In Tibet, Aksobhya is represented as *GAUTAMA BUDDHA*. He is usually depicted as blue in colour, and he is sometimes shown supported by a blue elephant. His main attribute is the thunderbolt and he is associated with the element. His *SHAKTI*, or corresponding female energy, is Locana. Aksobhya

AKSOBHYA (above), whose name means "Immovable", rules over the eastern paradise Abrihati, a land without evil, ugliness or suffering. (BRASS AND SILVER, TIBET, 13TH CENTURY.)

emanates the *BODHISATTVA MANJUSHRI*, the patron of the kings of Tibet. (See also *DHYANIBUDDHAS*)

AMITABHA is one of the five *DHYANIBUDDHAS*, and one of the most important buddhas of Mahayana or "Great Vehicle" Buddhism. His name means "Boundless Light" or "He Whose Splendour is Immeasurable".

Amitabha rules over the western paradise, a state of consciousness known as Sukhavati. Everyone who believes in the buddha is promised entry to Sukhavati, where they are reborn. Amitabha is thus a type of saviour who assures people of a life after death: individuals are able to achieve liberation through calling on his name, rather than having to endure countless rebirths.

AMITABHA (above) seated on a lotus flower, emits rays of golden light.

AMITABHA (left), who gave up his throne to become the monk Dharmakara, is shown here with a begging bowl. He achieved enlightenment and rules over the western paradise, Sukhavati. (GILT BRONZE, TIBET.)

In a previous existence, Amitabha was a king who, after encountering the Buddhist teaching, gave up his throne to become the monk Dharmakara. The buddha is thus sometimes depicted with a shaven head. Dharmakara took 48 vows in which he promised to help all those who attempted to tread the path towards enlightenment. Through meditation, the monk eventually fulfilled his vows and became the buddha Amitabha.

His element is water, and he is associated with the twilight and life in the beyond. He is usually shown as red in colour, sitting on a lotus blossom; sometimes, however, he is depicted riding a pair of peacocks.

Although he originated in India, Amitabha achieved his greatest popularity in China and Japan, where he is known as Amida, the buddha who inspired the "Pure Land" school of Buddhism. In the eighth century, the Indian monk PADMASAMBHAVA introduced Amitabha's cult to Tibet, where it also gained a wide following. In both Tibet and Nepal, Amitabha is often depicted in Yab-Yum, the posture of embrace, with his SHAKTI, or corresponding female energy, Pandara. (See also DHYANIBUDDHAS)

AMOGHASIDDHI is one of the five DHYANIBUDDHAS. He presides over the paradise of the north, and his name means "He Whose Accomplishment is Not in Vain".

Amoghasiddhi is sometimes identified with GAUTAMA BUDDHA and is normally coloured green. In Tibet, he is sometimes shown in Yab-Yum, the posture of embrace, with his SHAKTI, or corresponding female energy, Aryatara. The buddha sometimes sits on a throne decorated with garudas, eagle-like mythological birds. He may hold a sword in one hand and make the

AMOGHASIDDHI (above) one of the five Dhyanibuddhas, makes his characteristic mudra, or gesture, of fearlessness with his right hand. (BRONZE ENGRAVED WITH SILVER, 14TH CENTURY, TIBET.)

gesture of "Fear not" with the other. Amoghasiddhi's element is the earth and he is associated with the future buddha MAITREYA. (See also DHYANIBUDDHAS)

AMRITA is the elixir of immortality that features in the popular Indian myth of the churning of the ocean. The tale tells how, when the authority of the old gods was weakened, the *ASURAS*, or demons, began to threaten to usurp their power. The great god *VISHNU*, the preserver of the universe, suggested that the gods revitalize themselves by drinking the miraculous elixir Amrita, which they would have to produce by churning the celestial ocean. However, Vishnu said that they would need the assistance of the demons to accomplish the task.

In accordance with his instructions, the gods uprooted Mount Mandara and placed it in the middle of the ocean. Using the snake Vasuki as a churning rope, they whirled the mountain around and around until eventually it bored downwards into the earth, forcing the gods to turn to Vishnu once again for help. In his incarnation as the turtle *KURMA*, Vishnu took the mountain on to his back and the churning began again, this time more smoothly. However, the snake Vasuki began to suffer terribly and eventually poured forth venom, which threatened to engulf the whole of creation. *SHIVA* then came to the rescue. He succeeded in swallowing the poison, although it burned his throat, leaving a blue mark on his neck.

In due course, the ocean turned to milk and then to butter. By now the gods were growing tired, but they persisted in their efforts until at long last the water gave rise to the sacred cow Surabhi. After Surabhi came Varuni, goddess of wine; Parijati, the tree of paradise; the sun, the moon and *LAKSHMI*, goddess of wealth and good fortune. Finally, the divine doctor *DHANVANTARI* appeared holding the precious drink Amrita.

According to one version of the tale, the evil demon Rahu snatched the Amrita and began to drink it. Quickly, Vishnu chopped off Rahu's head in order to prevent the

AMRITA (left), nectar of the gods and the elixir of immortality, is held by the buddha Amitayus, sitting in meditation with the vase in his lap. (BRONZE, TIBET, 10TH CENTURY.)

AMRITA (right) came into being when the gods stirred up the oceans using the snake Vasuki as a churning rope.

elixir from spreading throughout the demon's body. None the less, Rahu's ghastly head remained immortal. According to another version of the myth, the drink penetrated throughout Rahu's body, whereupon Vishnu cut the demon into little pieces and set them among the stars. Yet another tale tells how the demons ran off with the sacred drink, whereupon Vishnu transformed himself into a beautiful woman, beguiled the demons and then succeeded in snatching the elixir back from them. The gods at last drank the Amrita and, having regained their power, drove the demons away.

ANANGA see *KAMA*.

ANANTA see *NAGAS*.

ANIRUDDHA, in Hindu mythology, is an epithet of Vahara, the third *AVATAR* of *VISHNU*. A *DAITYA* princess, Usha, fell in love with him and, assisted by her magical powers, brought him to her chambers. Hearing what had happened, Bana, the princess's father, sent his men to capture Aniruddha. The hero killed his assailants, whereupon Bana used his powers to kidnap the young man. When *KRISHNA*, his brother *BALARAMA* and his son, *PRADYUMNA* discovered what had happened, they determined to rescue Aniruddha. A tremendous battle ensued. *SHIVA*, the destroyer, and the god of war, *KARTTIKEYA*, both sided with Bana but, despite their help, Bana lost the battle. After acknowledging that Krishna was the supreme god, Shiva persuaded him to spare Bana's life. Aniruddha then returned home with the princess.

THE APSARAS, according to Hindu mythology, are heavenly nymphs who were originally associated with water and later with the countryside. According to the great epic, the *Ramayana*, their origin can be traced to the churning of the ocean (see *AMRITA*). When the Apsaras emerged from the water, neither the gods nor the *ASURAS* wanted to marry them, so they belonged to everyone and were known as the "Daughters of Joy".

The Apsaras are charming and beautiful dancers, and are said to be fond of games of chance. However, according to one tradition, they can also cause madness. They are sometimes said to live in fig trees and banana plants.

One myth tells how when King Pururavas was out hunting one day, he heard cries for help and discovered that two Apsaras were being carried off by demons. The king rescued the Apsaras and, struck by their beauty, begged one of them, Urvasi, to become his lover. Urvasi agreed on condition that she was never forced to see the king's naked body.

After living together for a while, Urvasi discovered she was pregnant. By this time, however, the *GANDHARVAS*, the friends of the Apsaras, missed Urvasi and hatched a plot, which would enable her to return to them. Urvasi possessed two pet lambs,

which she kept by her bed at night. One evening, the Gandharvas approached Urvasi and Pururavas as they lay sleeping, and stole one of the lambs. Urvasi loudly protested that she was shocked that anyone had managed to steal her lamb when "a man and a hero" lay next to her. The Gandharvas then took Urvasi's second lamb, whereupon she made the same comment. This time, Pururavas leapt out of bed, unable to bear the suggestion that he was not a man, and went to catch the thieves. The Gandharvas then lit up the sky with flashes of lightning so that Urvasi saw the naked body of her husband. At once, as she had sworn, she disappeared.

Pururavas set off in pursuit of Urvasi and eventually found her as one of a flock of swans, swimming on a lake with other Apsaras. He begged Urvasi to return to him, but she refused. Eventually she promised him that he could spend the last night of the year with her, in order that he might see his son.

On the last night of the year, the Gandharvas took Pururavas to a golden palace and brought Urvasi to him. Urvasi told him that, the following morning, the Gandharvas would grant him a wish. When Pururavas asked Urvasi what she thought he should ask for, she told him that he should seek to become a Gandharva.

The next morning, Pururavas did as Urvasi had advised. The Gandharvas gave him some sacred fire in a dish and said he must return home and offer up sacrifices. Back at home, Pururavas neglected the fire for a moment and it disappeared. One tree grew where he had left the fire, and another where he had left the dish. The Gandharvas told him that he should make another fire by rubbing together two pieces of wood, one from each tree. Having made the fire, Pururavas cast his offerings into it and achieved his wish to become a Gandharva. He lived with Urvasi ever after.

Another Apsara, Shakuntala, the mother of King Bharata, was said to live in the hermitage of a *RISHI*, or seer. King Dushyanta fell in love with her and asked her to marry him, then gave her a ring and returned home. Shakuntala, dreaming of her love, forgot to look after one of the hermitage's guests. In punishment, the guest told her that unless she journeyed to find Dushyanta and showed him her ring, the king would fall out of love with her. On her way to find the king, Shakuntala lost the ring in a lake, where it was swallowed by a fish. The fish was later caught and sold to the king who then remembered the Apsara and sent for her to come and live with him.

THE APSARAS, or "Daughters of Joy", are invoked at weddings to bring good fortune. They are dancers in Indra's heaven. (ANGKOR WAT, CAMBODIA, 12TH CENTURY.)

ARJUNA, the Hindu hero, was the son of the great god *INDRA* and Kunti, the wife of Pandu. Although Kunti was married to Pandu, he was under a curse and could not father children. Kunti conceived Arjuna and the other *PANDAVA* heroes after worshipping a variety of different gods.

ARJUNA is best known for his role in the *Bhagavad Gita* or "Song of the Lord", part of the Hindu epic, the *Mahabharata*. While waiting for the start of the great battle of Kurukshetra, Arjuna was troubled by the thought of the bloodshed and suffering that would ensue, especially since his opponents, the Kauravas, were his relatives. *KRISHNA*, the eighth *AVATAR* of the great god *VISHNU*, disguised himself as Arjuna's charioteer, and offered the hero comfort and spiritual teaching. He then urged Arjuna to do his duty as a kshatriya, or member of the warrior caste. Arjuna, overwhelmed with awe and devotion, was filled with renewed resolution. On another occasion, Arjuna and Krishna helped the fire god *AGNI* recover his power by burning down a huge forest.

ARUNA see *GARUDA*.

ASANGA see *MAITREYA*.

THE ASURAS, according to early Indian mythology, were beings who possessed supernatural or divine power. They were power-seeking and dangerous, and were opposed to the gods, or *DEVAS*. They are sometimes misleadingly described as demons, though they were not necessarily evil.

According to later Hindu texts, the creator being *PRAJAPATI* was the ancestor of both the devas and the asuras. The devas chose to follow truth, and the asuras chose to follow falsehood. At first, the asuras became rich through telling lies,

ARJUNA (left) the archer, a Pandava prince, rides into the battle of Kurukshetra against the Kauravas, which ended with the total destruction of both armies.

ARJUNA (above) and Krishna, the eighth avatar of the great god Vishnu, sound their transcendental conch shells. Krishna is disguised as Arjuna's charioteer.

but eventually they were destroyed. Occasionally, the devas were obliged to join forces with the asuras – as, for instance, during the churning of the ocean, when the gods sought to obtain *AMRITA*, the elixir of immortality.

One famous asura, Jalamdhara, was the product of the union of *GANGA*, the goddess of the river Ganges, with the ocean. There came a time when the power of the war god *INDRA* rose to equal that of *SHIVA*. Feeling threatened, Shiva manifested a towering form of anger and ordered it to wed the goddess Ganga to the ocean. The asura Jalamdhara was produced from their union, and *BRAHMA*

bestowed upon him the ability to conquer the gods. Jalamdhara performed countless miracles in his youth before marrying Vrinda, the daughter of a nymph. He then gathered together an army of asuras and declared war on the gods.

A tremendous battle ensued and the great asura even succeeded in overcoming *VISHNU*, although the goddess *LAKSHMI* persuaded Jalamdhara to spare his life. Eventually, Jalamdhara succeeded in driving the devas from heaven.

The devas sought help from Brahma, who directed them to Shiva. He advised the devas to combine their powers and to make a fabulous weapon, whereupon the

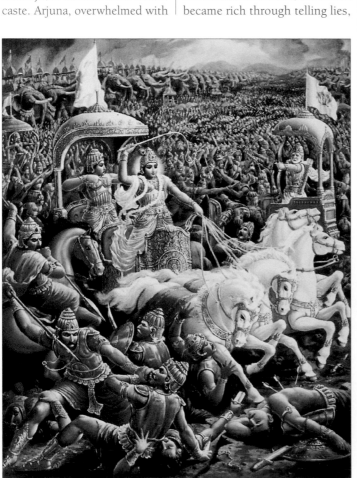

ARJUNA, having broken a vow he had made to his brothers, had to endure 14 years' exile. During this time, he journeyed to the river Ganges, where he became the lover of the river goddess Ganga. She gave him the power to become invisible in water. (PAINTING BY WARWICK GOBLE.)

devas forged a huge and dazzling disc, so bright that no-one could look at it.

Meanwhile, Jalamdhara tried to seduce Shiva's wife, PARVATI, although the goddess managed to escape him. Vishnu then disguised himself as Jalamdhara and succeeded in seducing Vrinda. When Vrinda realized what had happened, she died of grief.

Jalamdhara was furious. He resurrected his dead asuras and summoned them to battle once

more. Shiva threw the marvellous disc at Jalamdhara, cutting off his head. However, the asura simply grew a new head in the old one's place each time Shiva beheaded him. Eventually, Shiva summoned the wives of the gods. Taking the form of monstrous ogres, the goddesses drank all the asuras' blood, whereupon the gods won the battle and regained their kingdom.

The Hindu epic the *Mahabharata* tells how Brahma granted three DAITYAS – asuras descended from Diti – permission to establish three cities: one of gold in heaven, one of silver in the air and one of iron on earth. The three brothers ruled over them for many years. Countless asuras flocked to the cities where they were provided with their every desire. Eventually,

Shiva burned the three cities to the ground, together with all the asuras, and threw them into the depths of the ocean.

THE ASVINS, or "Horse Drivers", according to Hindu mythology, are golden-coloured twins who drive a three-wheeled golden chariot drawn by horses or birds. Known individually as Nasatya and Dasra, they bring divine bliss to humankind, and symbolize strength and energy. The offspring of the sun and the cloud goddess Saranyu, the Asvins are both married to daughters of the light. Each morning, they make a path through the clouds for the dawn goddess USHAS and scatter the dew with their whips.

In the *Rig Veda*, the ancient Hindu hymns, the Asvins often intervene with the gods on behalf of humankind. They also guard the RISHIS, or seers, from drowning in the sea of ignorance. The doctors of the gods, they are friends of the sick and unfortunate. They heal the blind and the lame, and rejuvenate the aged. They are chiefly associated with the war god INDRA and prepare the equipment of the warrior gods.

THE ASURAS, outwitted by Vishnu, chose to hold the head end of the serpent Vasuki during the churning of the ocean, and were nearly suffocated by the creature's hot breath. (KANGRA MINIATURE, 18TH CENTURY.)

Although they are kind and beautiful, the gods originally forbade the Asvins entry to heaven. However, the rishi Syavana eventually came to their aid. Despite being well advanced in years, Syavana had a beautiful young wife, Sukanya. One day, the twins saw her bathing in a river and, after flattering her, tried to persuade her to leave her husband for one of them. Sukanya refused, whereupon the twins said that they would make Syavana young and beautiful again and that Sukanya should then choose from among the three of them. Syavana agreed and, after bathing in the river, the three men emerged, all looking young and handsome. Sukanya took a long time to come to a decision, but finally chose to stay with her husband. Syavana was delighted: not only had he kept his wife, but he had regained his youth and beauty. In gratitude, he persuaded Indra to allow the Asvins into heaven.

MYTHICAL MOUNTAINS

THE VAST MOUNTAIN RANGE OF THE Himalayas inspired awe in all those who beheld it. Its peaks appeared to reach up out of the human world to touch the realms of the gods, and the range was regarded as sacred by both Tibetans and Hindus as a transitional domain between the human and the heavenly worlds. Mount Meru, the mythical axis of the cosmos, lay at its centre. One legend credited the mighty god Indra with the formation of the mountains: it was said that they had been a herd of flying elephants who had displeased him. He punished them by cutting off their wings. All the gods were thought to make sacrifices on the mountains, but Shiva was particularly associated with them. Mount Kailasa was his mythological paradise and, as an ascetic, his deep meditation on this mountain ensured the continued existence of the world.

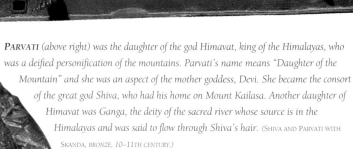

PARVATI (above right) was the daughter of the god Himavat, king of the Himalayas, who was a deified personification of the mountains. Parvati's name means "Daughter of the Mountain" and she was an aspect of the mother goddess, Devi. She became the consort of the great god Shiva, who had his home on Mount Kailasa. Another daughter of Himavat was Ganga, the deity of the sacred river whose source is in the Himalayas and was said to flow through Shiva's hair. (SHIVA AND PARVATI WITH SKANDA, BRONZE, 10–11TH CENTURY.)

MERU was supported on the hood of the coiled primeval cobra, Vasuki, who created earthquakes when he yawned and will consume the whole world with his fiery breath at the end of the present age. Both Hindus and Buddhists acknowledge the mountain's sacred status, and its shape is symbolized in conical objects of worship and meditation called yantras, on which the material world is depicted at the outer edge, and the absolute and eternal at the centre. (NEPALESE YANTRA.)

MERU (left) was the mythical mountain at the centre of the cosmos, the navel of the world, and was sacred to both Hindus and Buddhists. All the spheres of existence, from Brahma's heavenly city of gold at its summit, to the seven nether worlds at its foot, centred on the mountain, and the sacred river Ganges sprang from it. Its slopes glittered with precious stones and were clothed with trees laden with delectable fruits. It was surrounded by a vast lake and ringed with golden peaks. (MURAL PAINTING, WAT KO KEO SUTTHARAM, THAILAND.)

THE GODS (below) assembled on Mount Meru in search of the elixir of immortality, Amrita, which had been lost with other precious treasures in a catastrophic flood. Vishnu's solution was to churn the cosmic ocean until the treasures emerged. The gods uprooted Mount Mandara and set it on the back of the tortoise Kurma. The gods, with the help of the asuras, coiled the world serpent Vasuki around the mountain like a rope and each took an end. (THE CHURNING OF THE MILKY OCEAN, BASOHLI, C. 1700.)

MOUNT MANDARA (right), as it was spun, churned the cosmic ocean until it turned to milk, and then to butter. Eventually, the precious things it contained began to emerge: the sacred cow, Surabhi; the sun; the moon; Lakshmi, the goddess of good fortune; and, finally, the physician of the gods, Dhanvantari, holding the precious Amrita. The demon Rahu got hold of the elixir, but Vishnu rescued it by chopping off Rahu's head. The gods drank the Amrita to regain their power, and restored Mount Mandara to its proper place. (KANGRA MINIATURE, 18TH CENTURY.)

AVALOKITESHVARA is the most popular *BODHISATTVA* or "buddha-to-be" of Mahayana or "Great Vehicle" Buddhism. His name is translated as "Lord of Compassionate Sight" or "Lord Who Looks From On High". The Bodhisattva of the present age, Avalokiteshvara is said to have emanated from the great buddha *AMITABHA*. Although his residence is in Amitabha's paradise, he remains in this world in order to attend to the salvation of humans and animals. He is usually represented as a handsome man, with several heads and arms.

According to one myth, when Avalokiteshvara was looking down on the suffering in the world, his head burst open in pain. Amitabha put the pieces back together as nine new heads. Then, because Avalokiteshvara wanted to help all creatures, he grew 1,000 arms, and in the palm of each hand was an eye: "From his eyes were derived the sun and the moon, from his forehead, Mahesvara, from his shoulders, *BRAHMA* and other gods, from his heart, Narayana, from his thighs, *SARASVATI*, from his mouth, the winds, from his feet, the earth, from his belly, *VARUNA*."

Avalokiteshvara helps everyone who asks for his assistance. He visits hell to take cooling drinks to those suffering the heat of the damned, and he preaches the Buddhist law to beings incarnated as insects or worms. He is also said to protect people from natural disasters and to bless children. Moreover, the bodhisattva is said to have converted the female ogres of Sri Lanka and to have been given the task of converting Tibet to Buddhism.

In Tibet, his name is sPyan-ras-gzigs or *CHENREZIG*. In China, Avalokiteshvara developed into the goddess Kuan Yin, or Guanyin, and in Japan into the god, or sometimes goddess, Kwannon. (See also *BODHISATTVAS*)

AVALOKITESHVARA (left) is also known as Padmapani, or "Lotus-bearer", and holds a pink lotus blossom in his hand. In eastern religions, the lotus signifies non-attachment, freedom from ignorance, and the path to enlightenment.

AVALOKITESHVARA (above) the bodhisattva of universal compassion, is an emanation of the meditation of the Dhyanibuddha Anitabha, and therefore wears an effigy of the great buddha in his headdress. (BRONZE, 14TH CENTURY.)

THE AVATARS of *VISHNU* are his incarnations on earth in order to help humankind in moments of great crisis. It is generally accepted that Vishnu has ten avatars, although their number varies, and their identities are also flexible. Usually, the incarnations are said to consist of Matsya, *KURMA*, Varaha, *NARASIMHA*, Vamana, Parashurama, *RAMA*, *KRISHNA*, *GAUTAMA BUDDHA* and Kalkin.

Matsya, the first avatar, appeared as a fish who protected *MANU*, the first man, during the great deluge. The second avatar, Kurma the tortoise, supported Mount Mandara on his back during the churning of the ocean. Varaha, the boar, rescued the earth. The story tells how the earth, lost beneath floods, had been captured by a demon, whereupon Vishnu, as the boar Varaha, plunged into the waters and traced the earth by its smell. He killed the demon who had captured the earth and raised it out of the ocean on his tusks. Vishnu as Varaha is depicted as a giant with a boar's head, carrying the goddess of the earth.

The fourth avatar was Narasimha, who killed the powerful demon Hiranyakashipu, an incarnation of *RAVANA*. The demon had persuaded *BRAHMA* to give him the power to dethrone the storm god, *INDRA*, and to send the sky gods into exile. The demon then proclaimed himself king of the universe. Hiranyakashipu's son, Prahlada, was, however, a devotee of Vishnu. This so enraged Hiranyakashipu that he tortured the young man in an effort to dissuade him from his worship. Prahlada remained unswayed. Hiranyakashipu then ordered Prahlada to be put to death, but nothing could harm the young man. Eventually, Hiranyakashipu flew into such a rage that he struck a pillar, saying that if Vishnu was so important and omnipresent, why was he not right there, within the pillar? Immediately, the pillar collapsed, and Vishnu emerged

in the form of Narasimha, a man with a lion's head. Narasimha immediately seized Hiranyakashipu and tore him to pieces, whereupon Prahlada succeeded his father to the throne.

Vamana, a dwarf, was the fifth avatar who came to save the world from the demon Bali. The sixth avatar was Parashurama. When his mother had impure thoughts, Parashurama decapitated her at his father's command. However, when his father granted him a wish, Parashurama asked that his mother be brought back to life. Later, when

King Kartavirya insulted his father, Parashurama destroyed the whole kshatriya, or warrior, caste to which the king belonged. He then ordered the brahmans to sleep with the widows of the kshatriya men, in order to produce a new and purer warrior caste.

Rama, the warrior, is the seventh avatar of Vishnu, and the god, Krishna, is the eighth. Vishnu was said to assume his ninth avatar, the Buddha, in order to mislead the sinful so that they would receive their just deserts. Kalkin, the final avatar, has yet to come. He will

THE AVATARS *surround this picture of the god Vishnu. Taking the form of various animals, the avatars appeared on earth to help humankind during times of crisis.*

(*JAIPUR, RAJASTHAN, 18TH CENTURY.*)

appear at the end of the present age, or Kali *YUGA*, to establish a new era. It is thought that he will take the form of a warrior on a white horse, or a man with a horse's head. Kalkin will put an end to the wicked, and everything will be reabsorbed into the "Absolute" until creation begins again. (See also *THE AVATARS OF VISHNU*)

B

BALARAMA was the elder brother of *KRISHNA*, the eighth *AVATAR* of *VISHNU*, and was himself regarded as a partial avatar of the great Hindu "Preserver of the Universe". When the evil King Kamsa heard of Krishna's amazing exploits, he determined to kill him. He announced a wrestling match, challenging all the local young men to try their strength against the champions of his court. Krishna and Balarama, eager to take up the challenge, immediately made their

BALARAMA holding a horn, with his younger brother Krishna, playing the flute. The brothers overcame the champions of the court of the evil King Kamsa. (PAINTING BY BECHERAM DAS PANDEC, 1865.)

way to the city where the contest was to take place. However, when it was their turn to fight, King Kamsa released a wild elephant into the ring. The elephant charged towards the two young men, but Krishna simply leapt on to its back, put his arms round its neck and squeezed it to death. King Kamsa then sent his two strongest champions into the ring, but Krishna broke the neck of the first and Balarama crushed the other so hard that his heart burst.

Krishna later killed King Kamsa, but Balarama was killed in a drunken brawl involving Krishna's kinsmen, the Yadavas.

BALI see *VISHNU*.

BANA see *ANIRUDDHA*.

BANDARA was the title that was originally given to important officials within the Singhalese kingdom of Sri Lanka. In time, however, the term came to be used for a group of gods who were considered superior to the lesser deities, or *YAKSHAS*. For example, the god *DADIMUNDA*, treasurer to the supreme god *UPULVAN* and protector of Buddhism, is held to be a Bandara. Very often, a principal local god will be known simply as Bandara.

BCAN see *BTSAN*.

BODHISATTVAS are living symbols of compassion. They choose to delay the moment of entering nirvana in order to help others along the path to enlightenment. (STONE, 2ND–4TH CENTURY.)

THE bDUD were the heavenly spirits of the indigenous Bon religion of Tibet. However, within Tibetan Buddhism, the bDud came to be seen as devils. They were said to be black and to live in a castle.

BEG-TSE, a *DHARMAPALA*, or "Protector of the Teaching", is a mythical warrior who is regarded as a symbol of the conversion of the Mongols to Tibetan Buddhism. He

on to his head. For several years, the river meandered around the god's tangled locks, until at last Shiva divided it into seven streams and allowed it to flow safely out over the world.

BODHISATTVAS are "enlightenment beings" who are destined to become buddhas. They put off the moment when they will enter nirvana and escape the cycle of death and rebirth, in order that they may help others along the long path to enlightenment. Bodhisattvas are thus living symbols of compassion.

According to Mahayana, or "Great Vehicle" Buddhism, human beings are sometimes able to enter paradise by means of a bodhisattva's merits and spiritual power rather than through their own, provided that they call on the bodhisattva in faith.

Bodhisattvas are usually shown robed as princes, wearing five-leaved crowns. *AVALOKITESHVARA* and *MANJUSHRI* are two of the best known bodhisattvas. (See also *BODHISATTVAS*)

BEG-TSE (above), flanked by dakini, supernatural beings who are said to devour humans. He stands in his characteristic warlike pose, with one foot on a horse and the other on a man.

wears armour and carries a garland of human heads. In Lamaism, he is a god of war. According to tradition, in the 17th century, Beg-tse sided with the Mongolian warriors and led an army of animals against the Dalai Lama. However, the Dalai Lama assumed the form of the *BODHISATTVA AVALOKITESHVARA* and converted Beg-tse to Buddhism.

BHAGIRATHA, according to Hindu mythology, was the sage who persuaded *BRAHMA* and *SHIVA* to send the sacred river Ganges down to earth from heaven. The earth had become littered with the ashes of the dead, and Bhagiratha realized that the waters of the Ganges would wash them away and liberate the spirits of those who had been cremated. In order to prevent a disastrous flood, the great god Shiva allowed the river to fall

BHAGIRATHA (below) endured rigorous austerities to induce the gods to allow the sacred river Ganges to flow down to earth, to carry away the ashes of his ancestors so that their spirits might be freed. (ROCK CARVING AT MAMALLAPURAM, INDIA, 7TH CENTURY.)

BRAHMA, according to Hindu mythology, was the creator and director of the universe. He was the father of gods and humans alike, and in classical Indian thought, he forms a trinity with *VISHNU* and *SHIVA*. The three gods are collectively known as the Trimurti. Vishnu and Shiva represent opposing forces and Brahma, the all-inclusive deity, represents their balancing force.

Brahma was also the personalized form of Brahman. Originally, this term referred to the sacred power inherent within a sacrifice, but it came to refer to the power, known as the "Absolute", which lay behind all creation.

While the god Brahma meditated, he produced all the material elements of the universe and the concepts that enabled human beings to understand them. In each day of Brahma's existence, the universe is created, and in each night, it is reabsorbed. Within each of these cycles, there are four successive ages, or *YUGAS*, beginning with the Krita Yuga, or golden age, and ending with the Kali Yuga, the present age of conflict and despair.

According to one myth, Brahma produced the beautiful goddess Satarupa from his own body. She was so lovely that he was unable to stop staring at her, and whenever she moved aside to avoid his gaze, he sprouted a new head in order that he might continue looking at her. Eventually, Brahma overcame her shyness and persuaded Satarupa to marry him, and they retired to a secret place for 100 divine years, at the end of which *MANU*, the first man, was born.

Another creation myth describes how, in the beginning, the universe was shrouded in darkness. Eventually, a seed floating in the cosmic ocean gave rise to a beautiful, shining egg. According to the sacred texts known as the *Laws of Manu,* "In this egg the blessed one remained a whole year, then of himself, by the effort of his thought only, he divided the egg into two." From the two halves, he made heaven, the celestial sphere, and earth, the material sphere. Between the two halves of the egg he placed the air, the eight cardinal points and the eternal abodes of the waters. "From himself he drew the

Spirit, including in itself being and not-being, and from the Spirit, he drew the feeling of self which is conscious of personality and is master." The egg finally revealed Brahma the god, who divided himself into two people, a male and a female. In due course, these two

BRAHMA, the creator of the universe. His attributes include a vessel containing water from the sacred Ganges river. He is attended by Hamsa, a goose or swan.

beings gave rise to the whole of the rest of creation. Another version of the myth describes how Brahma

BRAHMA (above) produced a beautiful young woman from his own body. Each time she moved to avoid his gaze, he sprouted a new head so that he might continue looking at her. (STONE, CHOLA PERIOD, 11TH CENTURY.)

BRAHMA (right) receives an offering in the presence of a sacred fire. In one of his left hands he holds the Vedas, the collections of sacred writings that form the basis of Hindu belief and religious practice.

Brahma is often shown with four heads and four hands in which he holds the four Vedas, the holy scriptures of ancient India. His other attributes include a vessel containing water from the Ganges and a garland of roses. He rides on Hamsa, a goose or swan. Brahma's wife is the beautiful *SARASVATI*, the goddess of learning and patroness of arts, sciences and speech.

THE bTSAN, or bCan, are Tibetan demons who live in the air and appear before human beings as fierce hunters who ride their red steeds over the mountains. Anyone who finds themselves alone in wild and deserted places may be killed by the arrows of the bTsan.

CANDI see *DURGA*.

CANDRA see *CUNDA*.

CHAKRA SAMVARA see *SAMVARA*.

came forth from the egg as the primeval being known as *PURUSHA*. This creature had 1,000 thighs, 1,000 feet, 1,000 arms, 1,000 eyes, 1,000 faces and 1,000 heads. In order that the universe might come into being, he offered himself as a sacrifice. The gods and the brahman caste came from his mouth, the seasons came from his armpits, earth came from his feet and the sun emerged from his eyes.

Brahma was also sometimes known as Narayana, or "He Who Comes From the Waters". In this guise, he was regarded as lying on a leaf, floating on the primeval waters sucking his toe – a symbol of eternity.

Brahma's following was probably at its height in the early centuries of the first millennium

AD, when he seems to have been the focus of a cult. Usually, however, he was regarded as less important than Vishnu and Shiva, the other two great gods. Today, there is only one temple dedicated to him in the whole of India.

Brahma's fall from supremacy is accounted for in a myth concerning the origins of Shiva. According to the tale, Brahma and Vishnu were arguing over which of them was the most powerful. At the height of their quarrel a huge lingam, the phallic-shaped symbol of Shiva, arose from the cosmic ocean, crowned with a flame. When Brahma and Vishnu examined the lingam, it burst open. Deep within it the gods found the ultimate creator deity, Shiva, and they had to admit his supremacy.

CHENREZIG, or sPyan-rasgzigs, means "Looking with Clear Eyes" and he is the Tibetan form of *AVALOKITESHVARA*, the *BODHISATTVA* of compassion. He is believed to be the protector of Tibet and, according to tradition, is the founding father of the Tibetan people.

One tale tells how the Buddha *AMITABHA* saw the suffering of human beings and created Chenrezig out of his compassion for them. The bodhisattva is said to have appeared on a small island in the middle of Lhasa and, on seeing the immense suffering of all the creatures who surrounded him, to have vowed that he would never leave the world until every one attained peace.

The innumerable creatures all begged to be given bodies. Chenrezig did as they requested and, in order that they might achieve spiritual liberation, he preached the Buddhist teachings to them. However, more and more creatures kept appearing. Eventually, Chenrezig despaired of ever being able to help everybody. He begged Amitabha to allow him to break his vow and, in despair, his body broke into countless pieces.

Amitabha felt sorry for Chenrezig and re-created him, giving him even greater power. The bodhisattva now had numerous heads, 1,000 arms and an eye in the palm of each hand. Chenrezig still felt daunted by the task that lay ahead of him and began to weep at the thought. From one of his tears, the goddess *TARA* was born, and together, they proceeded to help everyone attain liberation.

Tibetans traditionally regard their original ancestors as Avalokiteshvara in the form of a monkey and the goddess Tara (sGrol-ma) in the form of a rock ogress. One story tells how the monkey journeyed to the Himalayas in order to engage in a prolonged and undisturbed period of meditation. When he arrived at his destination, he was soon spot-

ted by a rock ogress. Although the ogress attempted to seduce the monkey, none of her charms succeeded in persuading him to break his vow of chastity. The ogress became so frustrated and angry that it seemed that she might be about to destroy the world, whereupon the monkey finally gave in to her entreaties. The couple eventually produced six children. From these children, the entire population of Tibet arose.

King Songtsen Gampo (AD 620–49), who was responsible for the introduction of Buddhism to Tibet, is traditionally said to have been an incarnation of Chenrezig. The Dalai Lama is also regarded as an incarnation of the bodhisattva.

CUNDA, or Candra, or Cundi, is a *BODHISATTVA*, regarded either as a female form of *AVALOKITESHVARA* or as an emanation of Vajrasattva or *VAIROCANA*, whose image she

CHENREZIG, the bodhisattva, is the protector of Tibet and is believed to be incarnated in its spiritual leaders.

sometimes bears on her crown. She is said to have given birth to 700,000 buddhas and is therefore sometimes referred to as "Mother of the Buddhas".

Cunda may have developed from the Hindu goddess of the dawn, *USHAS*. She has one face, numerous arms and is coloured

D

white, like the autumn moon, or green. She rides upon the back of a prostrate man. The bodhisattva is kindly but threatening and possesses numerous weapons, including a thunderbolt, sword, bow, arrow, axe and trident. However, two of her hands are held in the gestures of teaching and charity. Although she helps the good, she is terrifying to the wicked. According to one Tibetan tale, she helped a warrior to destroy a wicked queen, who took a different king to her bed each night and killed him. (See also *BODHISATTVAS*)

CUNDI see *CUNDA.*

DADIMUNDA, or Devata Bandara, is one of the most popular gods of the Singhalese people of Sri Lanka. Originally, he looked after temples, but later he became treasurer to the supreme god *UPULVAN.*

Dadimunda finally emerged as the protector of Buddhism in Sri Lanka. He is said to ride on an elephant, attended by numerous *YAKSHAS*, or lesser deities.

THE DAITYAS, according to Hindu mythology, are giant *ASURAS* who oppose the gods. They are the

offspring of Diti, the sister of *ADITI* and one of the wives of the sage *KASYAPA* who fathered *GARUDA.*

HAYAGRIVA is a famous daitya who appears in both Hindu and Buddhist mythology. On one occasion, he attacked *BRAHMA* and stole from him the four books that make up the Veda, the "sacred knowledge" of the Hindus. *VISHNU*, reincarnated as the *AVATAR* Matsya the fish, managed to kill Hayagriva and retrieve the sacred texts. In

Tibetan Buddhism, Hayagriva was a lord of wrath, the leader of the terrifying gods known as Drag-shed (see *DHARMAPALAS.*)

Another daitya, Prahlada, was renowned for his devotion to Vishnu. According to one tradition, Prahlada was raised by Vishnu in order that one day he might become king of the daityas. Prahlada's father, the demon king Hiranyakashipu and avatar of *RAVANA*, was furious that his son

THE DAITYAS, with the other asuras, were persuaded by the gods to help them obtain Amrita. The daityas wanted to drink the elixir, but the gods offered them wine instead. When the daityas were all drunk, the gods made off with the Amrita. (ILLUSTRATION TO THE MAHABHARATA.)

worshipped Vishnu, but eventually Vishnu, as the avatar *NARASIMHA*, killed Hiranyakashipu.

The Hindu epic, the *Mahabharata*, tells how three daitya brothers asked Brahma to grant them invulnerability. Brahma said it was impossible to do so, whereupon the brothers asked that they might establish three cities and return to them after 1,000 years. Brahma agreed. He told the great asura Maya to build the cities: one of gold in heaven, one of silver in the air and one of iron on earth. The three brothers then ruled over their realms, populated by countless asuras, for many years, until, eventually, *SHIVA* burned the three cities, together with all the asuras, and threw them into the ocean.

THE DAITYAS fought the gods for possession of Amrita, which the gods needed to restore their superior power. Here, it is carried by Brahma, in the midst of the battle. (ILLUSTRATION TO THE MAHABHARATA.)

BODHISATTVAS

BODHISATTVAS ARE FUTURE BUDDHAS. They have such compassion for humanity that they take a vow to attain enlightenment, not just for their personal liberation but to show others the path they have found. In Mahayana Buddhism, this means that, even though they have reached the threshold of nirvana, they delay their own freedom and resolve to stay in the world to help others. For them, their own achievement of nirvana is not their only goal. They perceive further stages of enlightenment to be attained on the route to becoming a buddha. Celestial bodhisattvas, such as Manjushri and Avalokiteshvara, are very near to becoming buddhas themselves, and they act as mediators between the buddhas and mortals. They are not monks, but lay figures who are often portrayed as princes, wearing elaborate jewellery and a five-leaved crown. The bodhisattva Maitreya is the buddha of the future, a benevolent character who will arrive on earth in about 30,000 years, when the Buddhism of the present age has expired.

PADMAPANI (left), the "Lotus Bearer", is an aspect of Avalokiteshvara, depicted holding a lotus blossom. The lotus is a religious symbol in both Hinduism and Buddhism; in the latter it represents those who have conquered ignorance and achieved enlightenment. Padmapani is associated with the colours red and white, and wears an image of the buddha Amitabha on his crown, since Avalokiteshvara is Amitabha's attendant. (BODHISATTVA PADMAPANI, KHARA KHOTO, 13TH CENTURY.)

AVALOKITESHVARA (above), "The Lord Who Looks Down", is greatly revered in Mahayana Buddhism as the embodiment of compassion. He is sometimes depicted with as many as a thousand arms, all of which he uses to help humanity. The bodhisattva's compassion is so great that he even enters the realms of hell to alleviate the sufferings he finds there. In Tibet, where he is known as Chenrezig, the successive Dalai Lamas are regarded as incarnations of the bodhisattva. (TIBETAN STATUE, 14TH CENTURY.)

A MANDALA (left) has Avalokiteshvara at its centre. He is shown with many heads because he was so distraught by his vision of the sufferings on earth that his head split open with pain. In the mandala, a symbolic representation of the universe, the four walls and four open gateways are taken to include within them the whole external world, at the centre of which sits the bodhisattva in the position of lord of the world. (TIBETAN PAINTING.)

MANJUSHRI (above), the great bodhisattva, personifies wisdom and learning. The sword he wields in his right hand is used to cut through the veil of ignorance. In his left hand he carries a lotus blossom, holding a scroll which contains the "Perfection of Wisdom": these writings describe the ideal of the bodhisattva as the highest aspiration of religious life, and the emptiness of phenomena which characterizes Mahayana Buddhism. (CHINESE, 15TH CENTURY.)

CUNDA (left) is a female bodhisattva, sometimes called the "Mother of the Buddhas". She is said to be kindly to the good but terrifying to the wicked: she is portrayed with as many as 16 arms, each of which holds a threatening weapon, but for a worshipper who knows how to regard her, her hands are in the positions of teaching and charity. (RELIEF FROM CENTRAL INDIA, 10TH CENTURY.)

VAJRAPANI (left), the indigo bodhisattva, is one of the most important wrathful deities. Vajrapani is the destroyer of evil. His fierce demeanour represents the attitude needed to turn hatred against itself and transcend it. He is armed with a Vajra, or thunderbolt, which is the weapon of the Hindu gods Indra and Karttikeya. Vajrapani is also said to be the embodiment of skilful actions. (TIBETAN PAINTING.)

THE DAKINI, according to traditional Buddhist belief, are supernatural beings, or low-ranking goddesses. They fly through the air and are said to eat human beings. The dakini have magical powers and are able to initiate novices into the secret wisdom of the Tantra, a series of ritual texts dealing with the attainment of enlightenment. They can also help Yogis who wish to further their spiritual progress since they are able to concentrate the powers that the Yogi releases.

The dakini are usually shown dancing and appear as young naked women, as horrible monsters, or with the heads of lions or birds and the faces of horses or dogs. They also feature in Hindu mythology, as witch attendants on the goddess KALI.

In Tibetan Buddhism, dakinis are known as khadromas, female beings who move in celestial space. Their nakedness symbolizes their knowledge of perfect truth. The khadromas are said to live in Urgyen, a mythical realm that is also regarded as the birthplace of PADMASAMBHAVA, one of the founders of Tibetan Buddhism. In Tibet, eight goddesses, represented as beautiful young women, are sometimes included within the group of dakinis. They are known as the "Eight Mothers" and are thought to have developed from Tibetan shamanism.

DAKSHA, according to Hindu mythology, is the lord of cattle and the son of the mother goddess ADITI. He chose Sati, one of his 60 beautiful daughters, to be the wife of the great god, SHIVA. One tale tells how Daksha prepared an important sacrifice to which he invited all the gods, including INDRA. However, he failed to invite Shiva. Sati was outraged at this slight to her husband but decided that, even if her husband were not invited, she herself would attend the ceremony. Shiva was highly impressed by his wife's loyalty. However, he told her that Daksha was sure to insult him and that she must be strong and not respond to his insults.

When Sati arrived at her father's house, Daksha immediately began to insult Shiva, scorning his wild dancing and his appearance. Sati, finally overwhelmed with fury, denounced her father in front of all the gods. Then, since she had broken her promise to Shiva, she threw herself on to the sacrificial fire and was burnt to death.

Shiva was so angry and distraught at this turn of events that he sent one of his emanations, a terrifying demon, to kill everyone who had attended the ceremony. At length, the great god VISHNU, the preserver of the universe, persuaded Shiva to bring the guests back to life. Daksha finally acknowledged that Shiva was indeed a great god, and as a sign that he recognized his own stupidity he adopted the head of a goat. Shiva entered into a deep and prolonged meditation and awaited the time when Sati would be reincarnated as PARVATI.

In another version of the myth, Daksha's head was torn off, and Sati was brought back to life after the massacre. The goddess begged Shiva to restore her father to life. The great god agreed but, because nobody could find Daksha's head, he was given that of a ram.

THE DANAVAS are half-divine, half-demonic beings of Hindu mythology who were banished by the war god, INDRA, to live in the ocean. The monster Bali, whom it is said that VISHNU overcame in his incarnation as Vamana the dwarf, was a danava. The danavas were ASURAS, and although they are often described as "demons", they were not totally evil.

Vishnu, for example, recognized that Bali had shown himself to be capable of honourable behaviour and so rewarded him by making him king of the underworld.

DASRA see ASVINS.

DEVADATTA was a cousin of GAUTAMA BUDDHA. He became a member of the Buddhist community but grew jealous of Gautama and planned to murder him. First of all, he sent a group of assassins to murder the great teacher. However, the men were so impressed by the Buddha that they repented their evil intentions and became his followers. Then, Devadatta tried to crush Gautama by rolling an enormous boulder on

DHANVANTARI features in the ancient Indian myth of the churning of the ocean. It was he who appeared bearing *AMRITA*, the elixir of immortality, from the milk ocean. Dhanvantari was also known as Sudapani, or "One Who Bears Nectar in His Hands". The master of universal knowledge, he came to be regarded as the physician of the gods. He is the guardian deity of hospitals which are usually in the vicinity of a sanctuary of *VISHNU*.

top of him. However, the boulder stopped before it reached its target. Finally, he sent a wild elephant to gore the Buddha to death. The elephant was, however, tamed by the Buddha's kindness. When he died, Devadatta was condemned to lengthy sufferings in hell.

DEVAKI see *KRISHNA*.

DEVI (above), the great Hindu goddess, is the subject of an attempted seduction by her husband Shiva. On the right, he praises her for having resisted temptation. (SANDSTONE, CAMBODIA, 13TH CENTURY.)

DEVI (left) is honoured by the Hindu gods, Shiva, Vishnu, Brahma, Ganesha and Indra. (ILLUSTRATION BY J. HIGGINBOTHAM, 1864.)

THE DEVAS are the divine beings of the Veda, the ancient sacred teachings of India. The devas were regarded as immortal, and their chief attribute was their power, which enabled them to help human beings.

They later came to be regarded as those gods who are less important than great gods such as *ISHNU* and *SHIVA*. Although they inhabit a realm higher than that of human beings, they are still mortal. Among these Hindu devas are groups such as the *ADITYAS*, the rudras and the vasus.

In Buddhism, the devas are divine beings who live in the celestial heavens but are none the less subject to the ongoing cycle of death and rebirth. Most of the Buddhist devas originated in the Indian pantheon. They have long, pleasurable lives, and promote and protect Buddhism.

DEVATA BANDARA see *DADIMUNDA*.

DEVI is an aspect of the "Great Goddess" in Hindu mythology. It is the name by which the god *SHIVA*'s wife is sometimes known and is also the name given to female Hindu deities in general. Devi, as Shiva's *SHAKTI*, or consort, is both a benevolent and a fearsome deity, and is regarded as a major goddess within Hinduism.

She is a complex figure, taking many different forms, including those of *DURGA*, *KALI*, *PARVATI* and Sati. Sometimes, she also takes the form of goddesses who are independent of Shiva. Her main attributes are the conch, hook, prayer wheel and trident. (See also *THE MOTHER GODDESS*)

DEVADATTA, the Buddha's cousin and his rival from childhood, hatched a plot to murder him, but his hired assassins were all stricken with remorse as soon as the Buddha touched the wall behind which they were hidden.

THE DAKINI include eight Tibetan goddesses, of which images such as this one were used in rites of exorcism which drew on shamanistic practices. (CARVED HUMAN BONE, TIBET, 18TH CENTURY.)

33

DHARMAPALAS are "Protectors of the Dharma", or teaching. In Buddhism, particularly in Tibetan belief, they are regarded as ferocious divine beings who protect the faithful from the evil demons and bad influences which might thwart their spiritual progress. As such, the Dharmapalas are similar to the *GUARDIAN KINGS*. In Tibet, the Dharmapalas are worshipped either individually or in groups of eight, when they are known as the "Eight Terrible Ones" or Drag-shed. The eight are usually said to be *KALADEVI* (Lha-mo), *BRAHMA* (Tsangs-pa), *BEG-TSE*, *YAMA*, Kuvera (Vaishravana), *HAYAGRIVA*, *MAHAKALA* or Mahalka ("Great Black One") and *YAMANTAKA*. Vaishravana is also one of the Guardian or Celestial Kings.

In Tibet, the Dharmapalas are usually shown frowning, with tangled hair surmounted by a crown of five skulls. Most of them are in Yab-Yum, the posture of embrace, with their *SHAKTI*.

Some of the Dharmapalas were also Lokapalas (Guardian Kings) who existed in pre-Buddhist times as members of the Bon pantheon. *PADMASAMBHAVA*, one of the founders of Tibetan Buddhism, assimilated some of these ancient deities and transformed them into deities who protected the Buddhist law. However, some of the Lokapalas were adopted from the Hindu religion.

THE DHYANIBUDDHAS, or

five "Great Buddhas of Wisdom", are the five meditating buddhas who, according to some traditions, are said to have arisen from the primeval buddha, *ADIBUDDHA*. They are sometimes referred to as Tathagatas ("Perfected Ones"), Transcendent Buddhas, or Jinas.

DHARMAPALAS with ferocious frowns decorate these ceremonial weapons. They wear jewellery of writhing snakes and each has a third eye in its forehead. (NEPALESE RITUAL AXES, 18–19TH CENTURY.)

DURGA, mounted on a lion, in combat with Mahisha, the terrible buffalo demon who threatened the power of the gods. (PAINTING BY BIKANER, RAJPUT SCHOOL, 1750.)

The term Jina means "Conqueror", and refers to someone who has succeeded in overcoming the cycle of rebirth and suffering.

The Dhyanibuddhas are VAIROCANA or Mahavairocana, AKSOBHYA, RATNASAMBHAVA, AMITABHA and AMOGHASIDDHI. They are sometimes regarded as symbols of the various aspects of enlightened consciousness. On the other hand, they are sometimes believed to represent the body of the Dharma or teaching. Whereas followers of the non-Mahayana schools of Buddhism tend to venerate GAUTAMA BUDDHA, Mahayana Buddhists make any one of the five Dhyanibuddhas their chief object of worship. Occasionally, Gautama Buddha replaces Amoghasiddhi as one of the Dhyanibuddhas and sometimes KSHITIGARBHA is considered one of their number. (See also DHYANIBUDDHAS)

DIPANKARA, or the "Lighter of Lamps", was a Buddha of a past age whom Shakyamuni, or GAUTAMA BUDDHA, met in a previ-

ous life when he was the sage Sumedha. After having honoured Dipankara, Sumedha determined that he would become a Buddha himself. He became a BODHISATTVA, or "buddha-to-be", and passed through countless lives before entering the TUSHITA heaven prior to his final birth, to Queen MAYA. Dipankara recognized that Sumedha would become Gautama Buddha, and proclaimed his glorious future.

DITI see ADITI.

THE DMU were supernatural beings of the indigenous Bon religion of Tibet. They are said to have lived in heaven.

DRAG-SHED see DHARMAPALAS.

DURGA is the great Hindu mother goddess whose name means "She Who is Difficult to Approach", or "Inaccessible". She is an aspect of the SHAKTI of SHIVA, and can be terrifying and ferociously protective. She is usually depicted with a beautiful face and

with eight or ten arms, in which she carries various weapons given to her by the gods.

Other goddesses are often identified with her, including Candi, who protects against wild animals, and Shitala, who protects against smallpox. She also manifests herself as the bloodthirsty KALI.

Durga is said to have been born fully formed, ready to do battle against demons. When the terrible buffalo demon Mahisha threatened the power of the gods, not even VISHNU nor Shiva dared stand against him. However, Durga rose

to the occasion. The demon changed first into a buffalo, then into a lion, whereupon Durga sliced off his head. Mahisha then turned into an elephant, but the goddess cut off his trunk. Although he hurled mountains at her, Durga overcame the monster, crushing him and killing him with her spear (See also THE MOTHER GODDESS).

DUSHYANTA see APSARAS.

THE GANDHARVAS are a class of Hindu demigods who are said to inhabit the heaven of the war god INDRA along with the APSARAS. They are part human, part horse and, as nature spirits, are associated with the fertility of the earth. The gandharvas guard the SOMA, the sacred drink that conveys divine powers. Some of them appear at Indra's court as divine musicians and singers. According to the *Rig Veda*, the ancient hymns composed by Vedic Aryans who came to India from central Asia, at the beginning of existence a gandharva united with an apsara to produce the first pair of human beings, YAMA and Yami.

DURGA is a slayer of demons who threaten the order of creation. She killed Mahisha, who was invulnerable to man and beast. (ILLUSTRATION BY J. HIGGINBOTHAM, 1864.)

GANESHA is the Hindu god of wisdom and literature, and the son of *PARVATI*, the wife of the great god *SHIVA*. He is portrayed with the head of an elephant and a pot belly, a symbol both of his greed and his ability to dispense success. He has four arms but only one tusk. An extremely popular deity, he is invoked at the outset of new undertakings. He is regarded as the patron of business, and businesspeople hold ceremonies in his honour. He was traditionally the first scribe of the great Hindu epic, the *Mahabharata*. He was said to have been so keen to write it down that he tore off one of his tusks to use as a pen.

One myth tells how, when Shiva was away from home, Parvati grew bored and lonely. She decided to make herself a baby and created Ganesha, either from the rubbings of her own body, from dew and dust, or from clay. She later ordered the child to stand guard outside the entrance to her rooms. When Shiva returned home and tried to see his wife, Ganesha, not realizing who he was, barred his entrance, whereupon Shiva knocked his head off. Parvati was distraught and demanded that her son be brought back to life. The first head Shiva

GANESHA's (above) mount, the rat, was originally a demon, who was vanquished and transformed by the elephant-headed god. (STONE, 11TH CENTURY.)

GANESHA (below), patron of literature, with Sarasvati, goddess of learning and the arts, mounted on a peacock and holding a lute. (ILLUSTRATION BY J. HIGGINBOTHAM, 1864.)

could find was that of an elephant. Parvati was delighted. Ganesha subsequently looked after the ganas, Shiva's attendants.

According to another myth, Parvati invited the god Sani, the planet Saturn, to visit her son. However, she had forgotten how dangerous the god could be and when he looked at Ganesha, the child's head burst into flames. *BRAHMA* told Parvati to repair her child with whatever she could find, which turned out to be the head of the elephant, *AIRAVATA*.

GANGA (right) the personification of the sacred river Ganges, is usually depicted holding a waterpot and a lotus in her hands. (STONE, BENGAL, 12TH CENTURY.)

GANGA, according to Hindu mythology, is the goddess of the sacred river Ganges. Ganga is the holiest of the three great river goddesses, the others being Yamuna and *SARASVATI*. The confluence of the three rivers, known as the Tirtha, is regarded as particularly sacred and is situated at the town of Allahabad, where a great mass pilgrimage takes place each year.

Ganga is said to have emerged from one of *VISHNU*'s toes. Until her descent, she was believed to live in the sky, but when the earth became filled with the ashes of the dead, the sage *BHAGIRATHA* prayed that the gods might allow her purifying waters to come down to earth. The gods agreed. However, the descent of the great river threatened to engulf and destroy the entire earth, so *SHIVA* allowed it to land on his head as he sat meditating on Mount Kailasa. After spending several years in Shiva's hair, the river separated into seven different streams and flowed down over the earth.

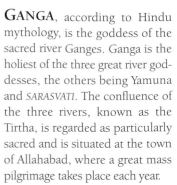

According to one myth, Ganga nourished the semen of Shiva in her waters, eventually producing the warrior god Skanda, also known as *KARTTIKEYA*. The tale tells how Shiva offered up six of his seeds to the fire god *AGNI*, who gave them to Ganga for safekeeping. Swaha, the daughter of a sage, visited the river on six successive nights and was impregnated by the seeds, eventually giving birth to Karttikeya. The child had six heads, and six or 12 arms and legs.

Another myth tells how *INDRA*'s power was beginning to threaten that of Shiva, whereupon a form of anger manifested itself before Shiva and asked that it might serve him. Shiva told the form to submerge itself in the Ganges and to marry the goddess to the ocean. A son called Jalamdhara, an *ASURA*, resulted from the union, and *BRAHMA* gave the asura the power to conquer the gods. (See also *SACRED RIVERS*)

GARUDA, according to Hindu mythology, was the prince of birds and the son of the sage *KASYAPA*. According to one account of Garuda's birth, Kasyapa had two beautiful wives, Kadru and Vinata. The sage promised to provide both wives with heirs. Kadru chose to give birth to 1,000 splendid serpents, whereas Vinata asked for only two sons. However, Vinata requested that her sons' strength and prowess should surpass that of Kadru's offspring.

Eventually, Kadru laid 1,000 eggs and Vinata laid two. After 500 years, 1,000 serpents emerged from Kadru's eggs. However, Vinata's two sons failed to appear. Impatient, Vinata broke open one of her eggs to find an embryo with only the upper half developed. The embryo became Aruna, the red glow of dawn. Aruna cursed his mother and ascended into the sky, where he remains to this day. Another 500 years passed and Vinata's remaining egg finally broke open to reveal Garuda.

Another tale tells how, in order to free herself from a curse, Vinata was forced to acquire *AMRITA*, the elixir of immortality and to give it to her nephews, the 1,000 serpents. Vinata asked Garuda to seize the drink from the gods and, after a mighty struggle, he succeeded in doing so. He put the drink down in front of the serpents, but said that they must purify themselves before drinking it. While they were busy performing their ablutions, *INDRA* retrieved the Amrita, as had been previously arranged with Garuda.

Garuda was a devotee of *VISHNU*, the preserver of the universe, and he was chosen by the god to be his mount. He appeared whenever summoned by Vishnu's thought, and fought with him against demons and demonic ser-

GARUDA, half human, half eagle, was the chosen mount of Vishnu, who rides him with his consort, Lakshmi, seated on a lotus flower. (PAINTING, BUNDI, C. 1770.)

pents. Garuda is depicted with the head, wings and claws of an eagle. In Buddhism, garudas are divine bird-like creatures.

GAURI see *PARVATI*.

GAUTAMA BUDDHA was the founding master of Buddhism and is regarded as the most perfect of holy men, rather than as a deity. By most accounts, he was born in the sixth century BC into the kshatriya, or warrior, caste at Kapilavastu, just inside the border of what is now Nepal. Gautama was the Buddha's family name; his given name was Siddhartha. In later legend he was known as Shakyamuni, or the sage of the Shakya clan. Gautama is venerated by all Buddhists, although for the "Pure Land" sect of Japanese and Chinese Buddhism, the Buddha AMITABHA, or Amida, has supreme importance.

The story of Gautama's life has become a legend. According to tradition, while in one of the Buddhist heavens, Gautama realized that the time had come for him to descend to earth. The spirit of the Buddha appeared in a dream to Queen MAYA: a small, snow-white elephant floating on a raincloud, a symbol of fertility, seemed to circle around the queen three times and then enter her womb. At that moment, all around the world, musical instruments played, trees and flowers bloomed and lakes were suddenly covered with lotus blossoms. Astrologers forecast that Queen Maya and the Buddha's father, the local ruler King Suddhodana, would have a son who would become either a universal emperor or a buddha.

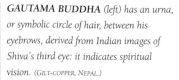

When the boy was born, he immediately began to walk, and a lotus sprang from the place where his foot first touched the ground. The child took seven steps in the directions of the seven cardinal points, and thus symbolically took possession of the world. Soon after his birth, his mother died of joy.

When Gautama was 12 years old, a wise man predicted that, if he were to witness old age, sickness or death, or to see a recluse, he would leave the palace in order to become an ascetic, one who shuns physical pleasures. In fear of the prophesy, the king surrounded his son with luxury and had high walls built around his palaces.

When Gautama reached the age of 16, he was married to Princess Yasodhara and 12 years later, their son RAHULA was born. At about this time, Gautama's curiosity about the outside world was aroused and he decided to set out to explore the land outside the palace grounds. The king immediately ordered that every sign of suffering and sadness should be removed from his son's path. However, on the first day of his excursion, Gautama saw a wrinkled old man; on the second day, he saw someone suffering from an incurable disease, as well as a funeral procession; and on another day, he came across a wandering ascetic. Gautama finally decided to leave home and become an ascetic. His father was devastated and provided even more amusements for the prince. However, nothing would deter the young man.

After six years of asceticism, Gautama realized that he was no nearer enlightenment than he had

GAUTAMA BUDDHA (left), seated in the witness attitude, is assailed by the powers of evil, led by the demon Mara. Demons in threatening human and animal shapes seek to terrify him, and Mara's daughters try to seduce him. (MURAL, AJANTA, BERAR.)

GAUTAMA BUDDHA (left) has an urna, or symbolic circle of hair, between his eyebrows, derived from Indian images of Shiva's third eye: it indicates spiritual vision. (GILT-COPPER, NEPAL.)

GAUTAMA BUDDHA (right), having decided to renounce the world, cuts off his hair. (TIBET, 18TH CENTURY.)

been while living his former life of luxury. Deciding that he must free himself from desire, he set off for the town of Bodh Gaya; as he journeyed, light radiated from his body, attracting peacocks and kingfishers. When Gautama reached Bodh Gaya, he sat down beneath the branches of a sacred tree, whereupon the earth shook six times.

While Gautama was meditating, he was tested by the demon MARA, the Buddhist equivalent of Satan. First, he was subjected to fear, then enticed with pleasure. However, Gautama remained unmoved. Eventually he became aware of the "Four Noble Truths" that became the basis of his teaching: that life is full of suffering, that suffering depends on certain conditions such as craving, that these conditions can be removed, and that the way to make suffering cease is to practise the eightfold path: right view, right thought, right speech, right action, right livelihood, right effort, right mindfulness and right concentration or contemplation.

Gautama had reached a state of perfection and at that moment attained complete spiritual insight. The earth swayed, breezes blew, flowers rained down from heaven, the gods rejoiced and all living things were happy. Seven weeks later, he preached his first sermon at Sarnath, on the outskirts of the holy city of Benares.

Gautama preached for more than 40 years, during which time he performed many miracles and converted all who heard him, including his father, his son, his first cousin Ananda, his wife and his adoptive mother,

several conditions that he set before the gods, believing that they would be impossible to fulfil. He demanded that his father should be a god and his mother a snake; that he should be given an immortal horse, which could fly through the sky and speak all languages; that he should be supplied with a magical bow and arrow and strong companions; that he should be given a beautiful wife, for whom everybody would be willing to fight; and a clever uncle, who would be able to assist him with battle plans. He also insisted that the gods should protect and help him at all times. To Gesar's distress, the gods agreed to all his demands, so he was forced to descend to earth.

The earthly Gesar was conceived when a god descended in the form of a rainbow and gave Gongmo – a NAGA who had transformed herself into a beautiful young girl – a drink of water from a holy vase. Gongmo became pregnant, and in due course, Gesar emerged from his mother as a globe of golden light, which eventually broke open to reveal a baby. According to some versions of the tale, the baby had three eyes, whereupon his horrified mother immediately plucked one out.

Having been warned that he would be overthrown by Gesar, the ruling king tried to kill the child almost as soon as he was born, but, despite his every effort, the boy remained unharmed. However, Gesar and his mother were forced into exile. At the age of 15, Gesar entered a horse race, and on winning it, was made King of Ling and given the former king's daughter as his wife. King Gesar then fought and conquered several demons and converted several countries to Buddhism.

He finally returned to heaven, although in the knowledge that he would have to return to earth one day. Gesar came to be regarded as a warrior god and god of wealth; his consort was a DAKINI.

MAHAPRAJ-APATI GAUTAMI. He even ascended into heaven, where he converted his mother, Queen Maya, before climbing back down to earth on a ladder, accompanied by the gods. At the age of 80, Gautama entered nirvana, the ultimate state of spiritual bliss, near his birthplace. (See also *THE AVATARS OF VISHNU; THE LIFE OF THE BUDDHA*)

GESAR was a mythical king who inspired the greatest epic of Tibetan Buddhism. Tales of his exploits began to arise in the 11th century, at the time when Buddhism was beginning to infiltrate Tibet and threaten the indigenous Bon religion. The legends describe King Gesar's battle against the ancient beliefs and are said to be several times the length of the Bible.

Gesar, whose name means "Lotus Temple", was said to have been born in the kingdom of Ling, in eastern Tibet. He is regarded as the embodiment of the *BODHISATTVA AVALOKITESHVARA*, as well as of *PADMASAMBHAVA*, one of the founders of Tibetan Buddhism. His warriors are said to be incarnations of the Mahasiddhas, great ascetics.

Although the stories about Gesar are influenced above all by Buddhism, traces of the Bon religion can also be found in the tales that tell of mountain deities and spirits of places. Travelling singers transmitted the early versions of the epic, whereas the later tales were said to arise from Tibetan monks.

The story of Gesar tells how an old woman died cursing all religions. Her final wish was that in a future life she and her three sons might rule over all Buddhist lands and wreak their revenge on the Buddhist teaching. The gods, hearing that the woman and her sons were threatening to return to the world as horrifying monsters, decided to send one of their number, Gesar, down to earth in order to do battle against them.

Gesar was reluctant to assume human form and so, before agreeing to descend to earth, he drew up

TIRTHANKARAS

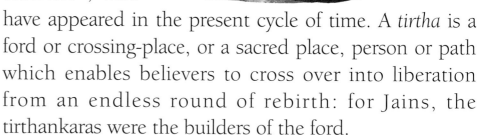

JAINISM IS AN INDIAN RELIGION and philosophy which offers an austere path to enlightenment. Much of its mythology was inherited from Hinduism, including huge numbers of gods, and ideas on the structure of the universe, but Jains differ from Hindus in that they do not believe in the idea of creation, considering that time is cyclic. Jain ascetics attempt to conduct their lives following five vows: to injure no living thing (because everything has a soul); to speak the truth; to take only what is given; to be chaste; and to achieve detachment from places, people and things. Their examples in following this discipline are 24 tirthankaras, or "spiritual teachers", who have appeared in the present cycle of time. A *tirtha* is a ford or crossing-place, or a sacred place, person or path which enables believers to cross over into liberation from an endless round of rebirth: for Jains, the tirthankaras were the builders of the ford.

RISHABHA (left) also called Adinatha, was the first tirthankara of the present cycle. He lived for an extremely long time, and was credited by Jains with the establishment of the caste system, the monarchy and the rule of law. He also organized the cultivation of the land, the pursuit of the arts, and taught humankind the 72 sciences, including arithmetic and writing. In Hindu mythology, he was a minor avatar of Vishnu. He is represented by the bull motif and is usually shown naked in a standing yoga posture. (TIRTHANKARA, SRI ADINATH TEMPLE, KHAJURAHO, INDIA.)

MAHAVIRA (above), the twenty-fourth tirthankara, was a contemporary of Gautama Buddha. At the age of 30, he renounced family life and embarked on life as a wandering ascetic. He endured 12 years of fasting, silence and meditation to achieve enlightenment, then spent the next 30 years preaching throughout northern India. He and his followers went about naked to indicate their conquest of passion, and he and other tirthankaras are traditionally portrayed with downcast eyes, dead to the world. (HEAD OF A TIRTHANKARA, STONE, 10TH CENTURY.)

THE TIRTHANKARAS (above) were all considered to have come from the kshatriya, or warrior caste, and were not deities but human teachers who had achieved enlightenment. Worship of their images focuses on their teaching and achievements rather than on themselves. They are all depicted as identical, except for an animal or other symbol which identifies each one, such as the boar that is associated with Vimala (top) and the goat that distinguishes Kunthu (bottom). (DETAIL FROM THE TWENTY-FOUR JAIN TIRTHANKARAS, BUNDI, C. 1720.)

PARSHVA (left) was the twenty-third tirthankara, born to Vama, queen of Benares, in the ninth century BC. He spent 70 years as a wandering ascetic before attaining nirvana when he died at the age of 100 on Mount Sammeda. His symbol was the snake, and he was often depicted under a canopy of cobras. He systematized the Jain religion, dividing its adherents into monks, nuns, and male and female laity, and giving his chief disciples responsibility for the Jain community. (TIRTHANKARA PARSHVANATHA, ORISSA, 11TH CENTURY.)

GNOD-SBYIN see *YAKSHAS*.

THE GNYAN are Tibetan spirits who live in trees and stones. They send plagues, diseases and death down on humankind.

GREAT BUDDHAS OF WISDOM see *DHYANIBUDDHAS*.

GRI-GUM, according to Tibetan belief, was a king who, unlike the rulers who preceded him, cut the magic rope that connected him to heaven. The first human ruler was said to have come down from the sky, landing on top of a mountain. At the end of his reign, he returned to heaven by means of a magic rope. The six kings who followed him did the same. However, Gri-gum, the eighth king, failed to return to heaven. During a duel, the air became so filled with soot that, unable to see while waving his sword around, he severed the magic rope. He was then killed by his opponent.

GSHEN-LHA-OD-DKAR, in the Tibetan Bon religion, was the "God of White Light" from whom all other gods emanated. When nothing else existed, two lights emerged; one was black and the other was white. A rainbow then appeared and gave rise to hardness, fluidity, heat, motion and space.

THE GUARDIAN KINGS (below) who guard the four quarters of the world. Acolytes of the bodhisattva Avalokiteshvara, they are said to have assisted at the birth of Gautama Buddha.

These phenomena merged with one another and formed a gigantic egg. From that egg, the black light produced sickness, disease, pain and countless demons, whereas the white light produced joy, prosperity and numerous gods. The gods and demons together gave rise to all kinds of creatures. These beings inhabit the mountains, trees and lakes of the land.

GSHEN-RAB, or Shenrab Miwo, is traditionally said to have been the founder of the later or purified form of the Bon religion of Tibet, which came into being after the introduction of Buddhism to the country. He is said to have come from a mystic land known as Zhang Zhung, and he came to be regarded as identical to *GAUTAMA BUDDHA*. Some scholars have also identified him with Laozi, the founder of Daoism. He is represented seated on a lotus.

THE GUARDIAN KINGS,

according to Buddhist belief, guard the four quarters of the world and protect the Buddhist law. They are said to live on the mythical Mount *MERU*, at the gates of the paradise of *INDRA*, the protector of Buddhism. The Guardian Kings are acolytes of the *BODHISATTVA AVALOKITESHVARA*.

Originally, they were regarded as benevolent, but they developed into menacing warriors. They are usually shown wearing armour and helmets or crowns. The kings are said to have assisted at the birth of *GAUTAMA BUDDHA* and to have held

up the hooves of his horse when he left the palace of his father for the outside world. In Indian art, they are usually shown riding elephants, whereas in Tantrism they are often shown trampling demons.

The chief Guardian King is Vaishravana, the guardian of the north and of winter. His name means "He Who is Knowing", and he is lord of the *YAKSHAS*, divine beings who protect and serve their ruler.

The guardian of the south, Virudhaka or the "Powerful One", fights ignorance and protects the root of goodness in human beings. He rules over the summer, and, in

Tibet, he is often shown with a helmet made from an elephant's head. The guardian of the east, Dhritarashtra, or "He Who Maintains the Kingdom of the Law", presides over the spring and maintains the state. The guardian of the west, Virupaksha, or "He Who Sees All" presides over the autumn. Virupaksha is usually represented standing on a rock or on demons, and wearing armour.

In Hinduism, the guardians are known as Lokapalas. Vaishravana is worshipped as Kuvera, a god of wealth who guards his buried treasure. Kuvera became the king of

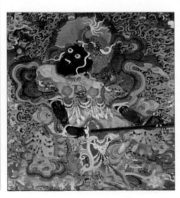

HANUMAN (above) wrestles with the demons of Ravana as he strives to find Rama's wife, Sita. (TERRACOTTA, 5TH CENTURY.)

HANUMAN (left), the Hindu monkey god, was well known for his extraordinary agility, which enabled him to escape from the demon Ravana. (JAIPUR, 17TH CENTURY.)

LANKA and drove a magnificent chariot, which the demon king RAVANA used in battle in the Hindu epic, the *Ramayana*.

HANUMAN

HANUMAN is the monkey god of Hindu mythology. He is regarded as the patron of learning and is the son of VAYU, god of the winds. According to one myth, Hanuman once tried to snatch the sun from the sky, thinking it was something to eat. To prevent the catastrophe, the war god INDRA threw his thunderbolt at the monkey, smashing his jaw.

In the great Hindu epic the *Ramayana*, Hanuman is the minister of the monkey king Sugriva and the loyal companion of RAMA, the famous AVATAR or incarnation of VISHNU, the preserver of the universe. Hanuman assisted Rama when the hero was locked in battle with the demon king RAVANA, who had run off with Rama's wife, SITA. It was Hanuman who discovered Sita's whereabouts, on the island of LANKA, Ravana's kingdom.

Hanuman's extraordinary agility enabled him to leap across the waters to the island like an arrow.

However, in mid-flight, a sister of the demon king caught Hanuman's shadow and managed to pull the monkey beneath the waters, where another demon tried to swallow him. Hanuman succeeded in escaping by stretching out so that the demon had to open her jaws, then contracting, so that he was able to leap from her mouth.

Hanuman finally found Sita in a grove of trees. Each day, Ravana threatened the goddess with torture and death if she refused to marry him, but Sita insisted on remaining faithful to Rama. Although Hanuman offered to carry her away, Sita refused to touch any man but her husband. As Hanuman left to tell Rama that he had found Sita, Ravana and his demons set his tail on fire. However, the fire failed to hurt the monkey god, who instead caused vast destruction on the island by swishing his tail from side to side, setting light to countless buildings.

Back in India, Hanuman encouraged an army of monkeys to build a bridge across the sea from India to Lanka, thereby enabling Rama and his troops to approach and attack the demon king. Rama rewarded Hanuman for his help by giving him the gift of eternal life.

Hanuman was said to be as large as a mountain, with yellow skin, a red face and a tremendously long tail. His roar was like thunder, and he flew through the clouds with a great rushing sound.

HAYAGRIVA

HAYAGRIVA is one of Tibetan Buddhism's DHARMAPALAS, or "Protectors of the Teaching". He is the lord of wrath, the leader of the terrifying gods known as Drag-shed. His name means "Horse's Neck", and he is small, with a pot belly and a horse's head. In Buddhism, Hayagriva is regarded as an emanation of either the buddha AMITABHA or the buddha AKSOBHYA and as the terrifying aspect of the BODHISATTVA AVALOKITESHVARA.

In a Hindu myth, Hayagriva was one of the DAITYAS, giant ASURAS who opposed the gods. He stole the Veda, the sacred knowledge of Hinduism, when it fell from BRAHMA's mouth. VISHNU, reincarnated as the AVATAR Matsya the fish, managed to kill Hayagriva and retrieve the sacred texts.

Hayagriva is also regarded as an avatar of the god Vishnu, who is said to have taken on this form in order to retrieve the Veda, after it had been stolen from the gods by two daityas.

HERUKA

HERUKA is a Buddhist deity, an emanation of the buddha AKSOBHYA. In Tibet he is regarded as one of the protective deities, or ISHTADEVATAS. Heruka is usually depicted with three eyes, wild hair and bared teeth. His body is smeared with ashes, and he holds a severed human head in his hand. The deity sits or dances on a corpse and is sometimes shown with his female partner, Prajna, with whom he creates nirvana (spiritual bliss). Heruka confers buddhahood and protects the world from evil.

The herukas as a group are terrifying energies who are usually portrayed with haloes of flame. They dance with their huge and terrifying consorts. The herukas exist in the head region, and meditators who achieve their level are believed to be capable of reaching a realm of the ultimate reality.

HAYAGRIVA, the leader of the terrifying gods known as Drag-shed, wreathed with his enemies' heads. (BRONZE, TIBET.)

HEVAJRA is a *YIDAM*, or tutelary god, worshipped in Mongolia, Cambodia, Thailand and Tibet. He is usually represented with four legs and eight heads; his body is blue, and his heads are different colours. He is sometimes shown alone, but often in Yab-Yum, the posture of embrace, with his *SHAKTI* or corresponding female energy.

HIMAVAT see *PARVATI*.

HIRANYAKASHIPU see *AVATARS* and *RAVANA*.

INDRA, one of the chief deities of Indian mythology, is a god of storms and war. He appears in the *Rig Veda* – the ancient hymns forming part of the Veda, the sacred knowledge of Hinduism – as the king of the gods. Indra is red or gold in colour, and is large, fierce and warlike. In his right hand he carries a thunderbolt, which he uses either to slay his enemies or to revive those killed in battle. He is said to ride through the heavens in a chariot, often said to be the sun. In later times, he was frequently depicted on the elephant, *AIRAVATA*.

Indra was born from heaven and earth, which he separated for ever. He challenged the old order and became the leading deity, a less remote figure than the Vedic god, *VARUNA*. Indra was best known as a destroyer of demons, who led the gods against the *ASURAS*. He fought and destroyed the serpent *VRITRA* with a pillar of foam and, in doing so, gave form to chaos, liberating the waters, generating life and causing the sun to rise.

On another occasion, Indra set free some cows which had been stolen from the gods. This myth is interpreted as symbolizing how Indra released the sacred force, or light of the world. Indra was also worshipped as the god who provided rain. As the bringer of light and water, he absorbed many of Varuna's functions, becoming a fertility god and a god of creation.

A vast drinker with a huge belly, Indra was also associated with *SOMA*, an intoxicating drink used in religious rituals. It was from Soma that the god was said to derive his special powers. After drinking it, he became so large that he filled both heaven and earth.

Indra's importance gradually declined. Although he remained a terrifying god of thunder, he came

to be regarded as a divine earthly monarch who reigned in Swarga, a luxurious heaven situated on the sacred Mount *MERU*.

According to one myth, it was Indra, rather than *VISHNU*'s *AVATAR* Vamana, who fought the demon Bali. While Indra was attacking a host of demons led by Jalamdhara, Bali fell, and a stream of jewels poured from his mouth. Indra was

HEVAJRA is the Buddhist equivalent of the Hindu god Shiva Nataraja. He is shown in Yab-Yum with his shakti, Nairamata, who stands on two corpses. (TANTRIC BRONZE.)

so amazed that he struck open the demon's body with one of his thunderbolts. The different parts of Bali's body then gave rise to the seeds of precious stones. Diamonds were produced from his

K

INDRA (above) is a weather and fertility god, and a leading Hindu deity. He is shown wielding a vajra, or thunderbolt, and is seated on his mount, the elephant Airavata. (11TH CENTURY.)

bones, sapphires from his eyes, rubies from his blood, emeralds from his marrow, crystal from his flesh, coral from his tongue and pearls from his teeth.

In a story from the Hindu epic, the Ramayana, Indra seduced Ahalya, the wife of the great sage Gautama. One day, when he knew that the sage was away from his home, Indra disguised himself, visited Gautama's wife and pressed her to become his lover. Despite his disguise, Ahalya immediately recognized Indra and, because she was curious about the chief god, she

the guru will be able to discern which aspect of the divine will be most useful to the disciple.

JALAMDHARA see THE ASURAS and GANGA.

JINAS see DHYANIBUDDHAS.

KADAVUL see KATAVUL.

KADRU see GARUDA.

KALADEVI, known in Tibet as Lha-mo, is the only female DHARMAPALA, or protector of the Buddhist law. She is said to have been created by the other deities and provided with weapons, in order that she might defend Tantrism, a tradition of gaining enlightenment through ritual practices. Kaladevi rides a mule whose

agreed. Afterwards, as Indra was leaving, he met Gautama returning. Realizing what had happened, the sage caused the god's testicles to fall off. Gautama then cursed Ahalya, condemning her to lie on ashes and eat only air until RAMA visited her. The gods later replaced Indra's testicles with those of a ram. (See also MYTHICAL MOUNTAINS)

ISHTADEVATAS are protective Buddhist deities or sacred beings who are especially common in Tibet. Ishtadevata means "Beloved (or Desired) Divinity".

Each individual who decides to enter the path of Bhakti yoga – that of loving submission to a deity – chooses their own ishtadevata. Alternatively, the individual's guru may choose the ishtadevata, since

reins are made from poisonous snakes and whose back is covered with the skin of a YAKSHA. According to one myth, the skin is that of Kaladevi's son, whom she is said to have devoured. Kaladevi has three protruding eyes, ten arms and, like all Dharmapalas, wears a crown and garland of skulls. She is sometimes said to be the wife of a yaksha king of Sri Lanka and is occasionally depicted walking on a lake of blood along with two other female beings. A terrifying and bloodthirsty goddess, she is often regarded as a consort of YAMA, god of the dead. She helps those who earnestly seek her protection.

KALADEVI, a bloodthirsty goddess who is the only female Dharmapala, or protector of the Buddhist teaching. (BRONZE AND ENAMEL, TIBET, 18TH CENTURY.)

KALI, the "Black One", is the terrifying aspect of the great mother goddess and *SHAKTI* of *SHIVA*. The personification of death and destruction, she is said to spring from the forehead of *DURGA*, another aspect of the goddess, when she becomes angry. Kali is usually depicted with blood-red eyes, four arms and with her tongue lolling out of her mouth in search of blood. She is naked, but for a girdle of severed heads or hands, a necklace of skulls and a tiger skin.

Like Shiva, Kali has a third eye in her forehead. In one hand she holds a weapon, in another the severed head of a giant, while her remaining two hands, in contrast, are raised in blessing. Her devotees regard her as a loving mother goddess who can destroy death as well as demons.

One myth tells how a monster, Raktabija, was destroying the world. Each time he was wounded, 1,000 demons sprang from each drop of his blood. The gods asked Kali to destroy the monster and, as she set about killing the demons, she drank their blood before it reached the ground, so that they were unable to multiply. When only the original monster remained, Kali gulped him down in one mouthful.

In celebration of her victory, she began to dance. As her movements became more and more frenzied, all creation began to shake, and the whole of existence was threatened with destruction. The gods begged Shiva to stop the goddess from dancing, but even the great god was unable to calm her. Eventually, Shiva threw himself on the ground in front of the goddess, whereupon she began to dance on his body. Finally, Kali realized what she was doing and stopped dancing.

The city of Calcutta is called after the goddess: its name means "Kali Ghat" or "Kali's Steps". Each day, animals are sacrificed to her, and it is believed that human sacrifices were made to her in the past. (See also *THE MOTHER GODDESS*)

KAMA, in the form of Kamadeva, is the god of love. Often depicted as a young man riding on a parrot, he bears a bow and arrows made of sugar cane and decorated with flowers. (ILLUSTRATION BY J. HIGGINBOTHAM.)

KALKIN see *AVATARS*.

KAMA, according to the ancient sacred teachings of India, is either sexual desire or the impulse towards good. However, Kama is sometimes regarded as a deity. Described as the first being to be born, he is superior to gods and humanity and, as a symbol of original desire, he is said to have brought about the created world.

In the form of Kamadeva, he is the god of love. He is sometimes regarded as the son of Dharma, god of justice and Shraddha, goddess of faith. Elsewhere he is described as the son of *LAKSHMI*, or as having arisen from the heart of *BRAHMA*. His consort is Rati, or "Voluptuousness", the goddess of sexual passion. Kama is said to rule over the *APSARAS*, the heavenly nymphs.

According to one myth, the goddess *PARVATI* grew bored because her consort, the great god *SHIVA*, was deep in meditation on Mount Kailasa. Parvati persuaded Kama to come to her aid. Kama was loathe to intervene, but Parvati insisted, whereupon Kama prepared to fire his arrow at Shiva's heart in order to remind him of his duties to his wife. The god Mahesvara saw what was about to happen; since it was

KARTTIKEYA, the Hindu warrior god, is named after the Kirttikah, or Pleiades. (SANDSTONE, PUNJAB, 6TH CENTURY.)

self-born, emerged from Time". One of his wives, Kadru, gave birth to 1,000 serpents, while the other, Vinata, gave birth to *GARUDA*, the bird chosen by the great god Vishnu to be his mount. Kasyapa is sometimes said to have fathered the *ADITYAS* by *ADITI* and the demonic *DAITYAS* by her sister, Diti. He is described in the Hindu epics, the *Mahabharata* and the *Ramayana*, as the son of *BRAHMA* and the father of Vivasvat, or the sun, who in turn was the father of *MANU*, the first man, from whom all human beings are descended.

In Buddhism, Kasyapa is one of the six Manushi, or "human", buddhas. He is the immediate predecessor to *GAUTAMA BUDDHA*. He is often shown seated on a lion, and is coloured yellow or gold because he represents the light of the sun and the moon.

KATARAGAMA DEVIYO is one of the four great gods of Sri Lanka. He is the equivalent of the Indian god *KARTTIKEYA* and the southern Indian Tamil god, *MURUKAN*. Originally, Kataragama Deviyo was called Ceyon, or "God with the Red-coloured Body".

KATAVUL, or Kadavul, is the name for the supreme personal being of the Tamils of southern India and Sri Lanka. The source of all existence, his name means "He Who Is". He is the judge of humankind, rewarding or punishing people according to their deeds during life.

KATUKILAL see *KORRAWI*.

KHADROMAS see *DAKINI*.

KHYUNG-GAI mGO-CAN was an ancient Tibetan god who may have been connected with the sun. He was said to have had the head of a bird.

KORRAWI is the Tamil goddess of battle and victory. She also takes the form of Katukilal, a goddess of the woods. The mother of *MURUKAN*, her temples are guarded by demons and spirits.

necessary for Shiva to finish his meditation in order for the cycles of creation to run their course, he struck Kama with a thunderbolt. Later, however, he brought Kama back to life. In another version of the myth, Shiva struck Kama with a flash of his third eye and burned him to ashes. As a result, Kama was sometimes called Ananga, or "Bodiless".

KAMSA see *KRISHNA*.

KARTTIKEYA, also known as Skanda, is a warrior god who campaigns against demons. The deity is sometimes said to have been raised by the stars of the Pleiades, or Kirttikah. He is sometimes also regarded as a god of fertility.

In the great Hindu epics the *Mahabharata* and the *Ramayana*, Karttikeya is described as the son of *SHIVA*. He is said to have been

KARTTIKEYA is sometimes shown riding a peacock, holding a bow in one hand and an arrow in the other.

conceived when Shiva offered his seeds to the fire god *AGNI*, who gave them for safekeeping to the river goddess *GANGA*. Eventually, a child with six heads, and six or 12 arms, was born.

Alternatively, Shiva is said to have directed the fire of his third eye at a lake. Six children emerged and were brought up by the wives of the *RISHIS*, or seers. One day, *PARVATI* hugged the children so tightly that they were squeezed together into one child, although the six heads remained.

KASYAPA was an ancient Indian sage whose name means "Tortoise". According to the sacred Hindu *Atharva Veda*, "Kasyapa, the

THE AVATARS OF VISHNU

THE GREAT GOD VISHNU WAS SEEN as the protector of the world, having measured out the universe in three giant strides and established it as the home of both gods and humanity. He was a benevolent deity, and his consort Shri, or Lakshmi, was the beautiful goddess of good fortune. In token of his willing involvement with the human race, he descended to earth and became incarnate at times when the world of mortals was threatened by evil. His incarnations, or avatars, follow an evolutionary pattern, from fish and reptile, through animals and the dwarf Vamana, to men and finally to the future creator, Kalkin. The number was traditionally fixed at ten, although the individual avatars varied slightly in different texts. The Buddha was assimilated into the series much later than the others, while the seventh and eighth avatars, Rama and Krishna, are important heroes of Hindu mythology.

MATSYA (above), the fish, was Vishnu's first incarnation. It was rescued by Manu from being eaten by a larger fish. Manu looked after it while it grew, then released it to the ocean. In return, the fish warned Manu of a catastrophic flood. It helped him build a boat on which he could save seeds and animals to repopulate the world, and towed the boat to safety. (ILLUSTRATION FROM DEVOTIONAL TEXT, 17TH CENTURY.)

KURMA (left), the tortoise, supported Mount Mandara on his back during the churning of the cosmic ocean. As the gods had uprooted the mountain and turned it upside down for this task, the peak drilled into the earth when the churning began. Vishnu, in his second incarnation as Kurma, dived underneath it and twisted with the mountain, acting as a paddle to speed up the operation. The milk ocean turned to butter and tossed up Amrita, the elixir of immortality. (ILLUSTRATION BY J. HIGGINBOTHAM, 1864.)

VARAHA (right) was the rescuer of the earth. The demon Hiranyaksha tossed the earth into the cosmic ocean, but in his third avatar, as Varaha the boar, Vishnu plunged into the ocean and killed the demon. He then found the earth in the form of a beautiful woman, whom he carried back up to the surface on his tusks. (BRONZE, GURJARA PRATIHARA, 10TH CENTURY.)

NARASIMHA (above) was the fourth avatar. Hiranyakashipu the demon, the twin brother of Hiranyaksha, dethroned the god Indra and proclaimed himself king of the universe. He was enraged by his son's veneration of Vishnu and condemned him to death, but failed to kill him. In his anger, the demon struck a pillar demanding to know why Vishnu did not show himself. The pillar split open, and Vishnu was incarnated as the man-lion Narasimha, who disembowelled Hiranyakashipu. (ILLUSTRATION BY J. HIGGINBOTHAM, 1864.)

VAMANA (above), the dwarf, rescued the universe from the demon Bali, who had assumed power over it. To release it from his grasp, Vishnu assumed the form of a dwarf for his fifth incarnation. He requested from Bali as much territory as he could cover in three strides. Bali easily granted this apparently trivial request, and Vishnu, transformed into the giant, Trivikrama, covered the underworld, the earth and the heavens in three vast strides. (ILLUSTRATION BY J. HIGGINBOTHAM, 1864.)

PARASHURAMA (above), although he was born a brahman, was destined to lead the life of a warrior. He was armed with a celebrated axe that had been given to him by Shiva. In revenge for insulting his father, he wiped out all the male members of the warrior caste and ordered their widows to sleep with brahmans to produce a new and purer caste of warriors. He was Vishnu's sixth avatar. (PARASHURAMA KILLING ARJUNA KARTAVIRYA BY CHAMBA OR BILASPUR, C. 1750–60.)

RAMA (left) was Vishnu's seventh avatar, assumed at the gods' request to destroy Ravana, the evil ruler of Lanka (the island of Sri Lanka). Rama, son of the king of Ayodhya, won his wife, Sita, by bending and breaking Shiva's unbendable bow. He was banished by his stepmother for 14 years to the forest, where Sita was abducted by Ravana. After many adventures, Rama killed Ravana, won Sita back, returned to his kingdom and reigned for 1,000 years. (ILLUSTRATION TO THE RAMAYANA BY MIR KALAN, C. 1750–60.)

GAUTAMA BUDDHA (left), Vishnu's ninth incarnation, was not identified until the third or fourth century AD. In the earliest accounts of it, Vishnu was said to have assumed this avatar in order to convert demons to Buddhist beliefs, with the intention of weakening them in their war against the gods, or to mislead sinful mortals so that they would receive their just punishment. Later, a more positive reason was suggested: Vishnu was said to want to abolish animal sacrifices.

KRISHNA (above), the god and the eighth avatar, was hidden at birth because of a prophecy that his mother's eighth child would kill the evil King Kamsa. Krishna was brought up in obscurity among a community of cowherds. After killing a succession of demons, including Vatsasura, who came in the guise of a calf, Krishna killed Kamsa. He assisted the hero Arjuna in the great battle of Kurukshetra, disguised as his charioteer. (ILLUSTRATION TO THE BHAGAVATA PURANA BY MANKOT, C. 1730–40.)

KALKIN (above) is Vishnu's tenth and final avatar, and is still to come: he will appear at the end of the present age, the Kali Yuga, which began in 3102BC and will last 432,000 years. In its final years, humanity will face a breakdown of civilization and a loss of spiritual and moral values. The divine incarnation of Kalkin, riding a white horse, will be needed to wipe out the wickedness of the world and establish a new era. (STONE CARVING ON PRASANNA CHENNAKESHAVA TEMPLE, SOMNATHPUR.)

KRISHNA, according to Hindu mythology, is an *AVATAR* of *VISHNU*, the preserver of the universe. He is traditionally referred to as the only complete avatar. A divine hero, Krishna is said to have been miraculously born in the town of Mathura in northern India. The gods wanted to destroy the evil oppressor King Kamsa, and so Vishnu decided to be born as the eighth son of the king's sister Devaki. According to one story, Vishnu plucked out two of his hairs, one black, one white. The black hair became Krishna and the white hair *BALARAMA*, Krishna's older brother. Krishna's name means the "Dark One".

King Kamsa learned that he was to be assassinated by one of his nephews, so he imprisoned Devaki and her husband Vasudev and killed each of their sons as they were born. When Devaki gave birth to Krishna, Vishnu told the couple to exchange their baby for the daughter of some cowherds who lived on the other side of the river Yamuna. The doors of the prison miraculously opened, and Vasudev carried the baby to the river. As soon as the child's toe touched the waters, they parted, allowing the father and son to pass through safely. Vasudev left the baby with the cowherds Yashoda and Nanda. However, King Kamsa discovered what had happened and sent a demon disguised as a nurse to look after the infant. Krishna sucked at the demon's breast until he drained her life away.

Krishna was a playful child, teasing

KRISHNA (above), an avatar of Vishnu, spent his childhood as the adopted son of cowherds. (KALIGHAT PAINTING, C. 1860.)

KRISHNA (left) is said to have taught the science of Bhakti yoga to the sun god, Surga, who instructed Manu, father of humankind.

the cows, laughing at his elders and stealing butter and sweets. He also displayed signs of his divine origins by, among other pranks, uprooting two trees at once; on another occasion, his adopted mother, Yashoda, was amazed to see the whole universe when she looked down his throat. Once, when the cowherds were about to worship the great god *INDRA*, Krishna told them that instead they should worship Mount Govardhana and their herds. The mountain, he explained, provided their herds with food and the cows themselves gave them milk to drink. Krishna then declared that he himself was the mountain. Indra was furious and sent down torrents of rain. However, Krishna lifted Mount Govardhana and held it above the storms for seven days and seven nights. Indra was so amazed that he came down from the heavens and asked Krishna to befriend his son, the hero *ARJUNA*.

One of the most popular myths concerning Krishna is that of his youthful dalliances with the gopis, the female cowgirls, and in particular with a girl called *RADHA* with whom the young hero fell passionately in love. Once, when the cowgirls were bathing in the river Yamuna, Krishna stole their clothes, then hid in a tree. He refused to return their garments to them until they came out, one by one, their hands clasped in prayer. Because all the cowgirls wanted to hold Krishna's hands when they danced, he multiplied his hands countless times. The sound of

Krishna's flute, calling the cowgirls out to dance in the moonlight, is believed to symbolize the voice of the supreme lord calling all who hear him to divine pleasures.

As Krishna grew older, he began to rid the neighbourhood of monsters and demons. Eventually, King Kamsa heard of his exploits and determined to kill him. However, Krishna not only succeeded in killing Kamsa but also went on to destroy numerous other oppressive kings as well as demons.

The most important battle he participated in was that of Kurukshetra. On the eve of the

KRISHNA visiting Radha, a young gopi, or cowgirl, with whom he fell passionately in love. His name means "Dark One" and he is often depicted as dark-skinned.
(ILLUSTRATION TO RASAMANJARI BY BHANUDETTA, BASOHLI, C. 1865.)

battle, Krishna, disguised as a charioteer, is said to have preached to the hero Arjuna the *Bhagavad Gita,* or "Song of the Lord", which forms part of the great Hindu epic, the *Mahabharata*. The war ended in the destruction of both armies, with only the merest handful of survivors on each side. Krishna died shortly afterwards. He was sitting in the forest, meditating, when a huntsman mistook him for a deer and shot an arrow, which struck him on his left heel, his only vulnerable spot. Krishna told the huntsman not to grieve or be afraid, and then ascended into the sky in a beacon of light.

Krishna is believed to embody divine beauty, joy and love, using his charm, playfulness and compassion to draw his devotees into the embrace of the supreme lord. (See also *THE AVATARS OF VISHNU*)

KSHITIGARBHA, who is a *BODHISATTVA*, or "buddha-to-be", is said to look after the six paths taken by souls after they have been judged. These paths are the destinies of humankind, *ASURAS*, demons, gods, animals and the damned. Patient and persevering, he consoles those who live in hell, seeking to lighten the burdens that they have brought upon themselves by evil actions when alive.

Kshitigarbha came to be regarded as the protector of all travellers. In India, he had only a small following, but he attracted many devotees both in China and Japan. According to one Chinese myth, he was a young Indian boy of the brahman caste who was so upset by how his late mother was suffering in hell that he determined to save all the other inhabitants of hell from such a terrible fate.

Kshitigarbha's name means "He Who Encompasses the Earth". In China, he is known as Dizang Wang, and in Japan as Jizo-Bosatsu.

KUNTI see *ARJUNA*.

KUN-TU-BZAN-PO, according to the Bon religion of Tibet, created the world from a lump of mud, and living beings from an egg.

KURMA, the tortoise, was the second incarnation, or *AVATAR*, of the Hindu god *VISHNU*, the preserver of the universe. During the churning of the ocean, Kurma supported Mount Mandara on his back in order to prevent the mountain from boring a hole in the earth. The gods were thus able to obtain *AMRITA*, the elixir of immortality, to restore their power. (See also *THE AVATARS OF VISHNU*)

L

KURUKULLA is a Buddhist goddess who emanates from *AMITABHA.* She is said to be able to cast spells on men and women in order to ensure that they serve her. In Tibet, she became a goddess of riches. Her main attributes are a red lotus, a bow and an arrow. She is often represented as reddish in colour, seated in a cave and with four arms. Her two upper arms are held in a threatening posture, while the two lower arms offer comfort.

KUVERA see *GUARDIAN KINGS*.

LAKSHMANA, according to Hindu myth, was the son of King Dasaratha and Sumitra and the half-brother of *RAMA*, an incarnation of the great god *VISHNU*. When Rama was exiled from his late father's kingdom, Lakshmana accompanied him on his travels. While the two brothers were living in the wilderness, Surpanaka, one of the demon king *RAVANA*'s sisters fell in love with Rama. He sent the woman to Lakshmana who in turn sent her back to Rama. The demoness, seeking revenge for being thus insulted, attacked Rama's wife *SITA*, but to no avail. Rama then asked Lakshmana to disfigure the seductress, which he did by cutting off her nose and ears. The demoness demanded that Ravana avenge her, and it was during this great battle that the demon king succeeded in abducting Sita.

LAKSHMI, or Shri, according to the Veda, the sacred knowledge of the Hindus, was alleged to have been many deities, including the consort of *VARUNA* or *SURYA*. However, she is best known as the beautiful consort or *SHAKTI* (female power) of the great Hindu god *VISHNU*. The goddess of wealth and good fortune, Lakshmi is usually depicted as a beautiful golden woman sitting on a lotus flower, the symbol of the womb, immortality and spiritual purity. During the Hindu celebration of Diwali, the

LAKSHMANA and Rama wandering in search of Rama's abducted wife, Sita. (ILLUSTRATION TO THE RAMAYANA, KANGRA, 1780.)

festival of lights, thousands of lanterns are lit and fireworks exploded in order to please the goddess. People gamble and feast, while the goddess is said to wander from house to house looking for somewhere to rest, and blessing with prosperity all houses that are well lit.

Lakshmi was said to have been born several times. For example, when Vishnu was incarnated as *RAMA*, Lakshmi was born as *SITA*.

Everyone wants to possess Lakshmi, but she insists that no one can keep her for long. She immediately leaves anyone who puts her on their head, which is what the demons do whenever they manage to catch hold of her. In early myths, Lakshmi was sometimes associated with *INDRA*, the war god. However, even Indra had to divide her into four parts in order to keep hold of her for any length of time. Lakshmi's presence is believed to bring fertility. According to one tale, when the goddess sat down next to Indra, he

began to pour down rain so that the crops flourished. Another myth tells how Lakshmi was born by her own will in a beautiful field, which had been cut open by a plough.

Lakshmi appears in the famous myth of the churning of the ocean. Using the snake Vasuki as a rope to turn Mount Mandara, the gods churned the cosmic ocean for 100 years. Eventually the ocean turned to milk and gave rise not only to *AMRITA*, the elixir of immortality, but also to the "Fourteen Precious Things", including the beautiful goddess Lakshmi, who rose seated on a lotus flower. The heavenly musicians and great sages began to sing Lakshmi's praises; the sacred rivers asked her to bathe in their

LAKSHMI (far left), laden with flowers, is a beautiful golden woman. Her presence is believed to bring fertility, and ancient Indian rulers would perform a marriage ritual in which they took Lakshmi as their bride to secure wealth and fertility.

LAKSHMI (left) sat on Vishnu's lap and refused to look at the demons who wanted to own her as goddess of prosperity when she emerged from the cosmic ocean. (ILLUSTRATION BY J. HIGGINBOTHAM, 1864.)

LANKA was the site of the battle between Rama and Ravana, the demon king. Ravana's horde of demons was eventually defeated by Rama's army of monkeys, assembled by Hanuman. (ILLUSTRATION TO THE RAMAYANA, RAJASTHAN, EARLY 19TH CENTURY.)

waters; the sea of milk offered her a crown of immortal flowers; and the sacred elephants who hold up the world poured the holy water of the Ganges over her.

LANKA was the old name given to Ceylon, now Sri Lanka. It was also the name of its capital. The walls of Lanka are said to have been made from gold by Vishvakarma, a creator deity and the architect of the gods. Originally, Lanka was intended as a home for Kuvera, god of riches, but the demon king *RAVANA* later captured it and took it as his own.

According to one tale, *VAYU*, a god of the winds, was responsible for creating the island. Narada, a sage, or *RISHI*, challenged Vayu to break off the summit of Mount *MERU*, the world mountain. *GARUDA*, the mythical bird, normally protected the mountain,

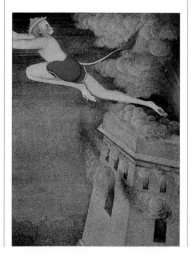

LANKA (left) burns as Hanuman, the monkey god of Hindu mythology, leaps across the water to safety.

but one day, in the bird's absence, Vayu succeeded in breaking off the summit. He immediately threw the summit into the depths of the ocean, where it remained as the island of Lanka.

THE LHA-DRE are gods, or supernatural beings, of the indigenous Bon religion of Tibet. When Buddhism entered Tibet, the Buddhist teachers assigned to the Lha-Dre the role of protectors of the new faith, thereby assimilating them into the Buddhist pantheon, where they are regarded as "Deities of the World" rather than the symbolic deities of Buddhism.

LHA-MO see *KALADEVI*.

LOKAPALAS see *DHARMAPALAS* and *GUARDIAN KINGS*.

THE LU are supernatural beings of the indigenous Bon religion of Tibet, who were assimilated into Buddhism as protectors of the faith. They live in lakes and rivers, and require regular placation.

MAHAKALA, or Mahalka, is known in Tibet as Mgon-po. The destructive form of the god *SHIVA*, he is one of the *DHARMAPALAS* of Tibetan Buddhism, and a *YIDAM*, a tutelary god of Tibet. He is known

as the "Great Black One", and has three eyes. He is covered with a tiger or elephant skin and holds a noose made from snakes.

His function, like that of all Dharmapalas, is to destroy all known enemies of the Buddhist teaching. Mahakala's most important duties are to pacify, enrich, magnetize and destroy. In the 17th century, he was accepted as the tutelary god of Mongolia, then under Tibetan influence.

MAHALKA see *MAHAKALA*.

MAHAMAYA see *MAYA*.

MAHAPRAJAPATI GAUTAMI was the stepmother and aunt of *GAUTAMA BUDDHA*. She raised him after his mother, Queen *MAYA*, died of joy a few days after his miraculous birth. The devotion of Mahaprajapati became legendary. After the death of her husband, Mahaprajapati persuaded the Buddha to allow her to found a Buddhist order of nuns.

MAHAKALA is a destructive aspect of the god Shiva. Threatening and armed with a sword, he is known as the "Great Black One". (TIBETAN, 19TH CENTURY.)

MAITREYA is the buddha of the future and the last earthly buddha. Regarded as the embodiment of love, his name means the "Benevolent" or "Friendly One". Maitreya is currently a *BOD-HISATTVA* dwelling in the *TUSHITA* or "Joyful" Heaven. In due course, *GAUTAMA BUDDHA* will enthrone him as his successor. Maitreya is expected to appear at the end of the present Buddhist age, in around 30,000 years' time.

Maitreya is often depicted as one of a triad with Gautama and the bodhisattva *AVALOKITESHVARA*. In non-Mahayana, or "Great Vehicle" Buddhism, the term *bodhisattva* usually refers either to Maitreya or to the historical Gautama Buddha, prior to his spiritual enlightenment.

The cult of Maitreya is very widespread in Tibetan Buddhism. According to one Tibetan tale, Asanga, a learned sage who founded the Yogachara school of Mahayana Buddhism, received his teaching directly from Maitreya. The Yogachara school teaches that everything consists of "mind only" and puts particular emphasis on the practice of yoga.

Asanga spent many years meditating on the future buddha. He eventually began to feel that his efforts to attain wisdom were fruitless and started to feel frustrated. One day, Asanga noticed that the wings of birds had worn a groove in a rock against which they always brushed when landing. The sage then heard the drip of water on a stone and saw that the drip had cut a deep passage through the rock. These two observations caused him to renew his determination to attain wisdom. However, though he continued to meditate, and though he continued to invoke Maitreya, he still got nowhere.

Some time later, while he was searching for food, Asanga met a man who was rubbing an iron bar with a piece of cotton. When Asanga asked the man what he was

doing, the man replied that he was making a needle. Once again, Asanga determined to continue his pursuit of wisdom.

Many years passed, and still Asanga had failed to achieve his goal. Finally, he decided to leave his cave for good. As he was making his return to the outside world, Asanga met a dog who was suffering excruciating pain from a wound infested with worms. Although Asanga felt great compassion for the animal, he knew that if he removed the worms, they would

die for want of food. Eventually, he decided that he would pick off the worms and allow them to eat his own flesh. However, he then worried that he might crush the worms, and so he decided to lick them off the dog instead.

Just as his tongue brushed against the worms, the dog disappeared and in its place stood Maitreya. Asanga asked Maitreya why he had failed to appear to him during his many years of meditation, whereupon the future buddha replied that only in this act of pure

MAITREYA (above) will appear far in the future, when India becomes an earthly paradise. (TIBETAN BRONZE, 11TH CENTURY.)

MAITREYA (right), the buddha of the future, and the last earthly buddha.

compassion had Asanga's vision been cleansed, although he had been with the sage throughout his many years of meditation.

Maitreya then told Asanga to carry him on his back into the city so that everyone might see him. Asanga did as instructed, but

MANJUSHRI, enthroned and surrounded by deities, is flanked by two lotus blossoms, on which rest a sword of wisdom and the Prajnaparamita-sutra, a holy text that advocates the ideal of the bodhisattva. (TIBETAN PAINTING.)

another tradition, Manu was the son of the sun god SURYA. Manu was saved from a cataclysmic flood by Matsya, an AVATAR or incarnation of the great god VISHNU, the pre-server of the universe.

One day, Manu was washing in the river when he found a tiny fish, Matsya, which begged the sage to protect it. Manu took the fish home, where it grew bigger and bigger until eventually it asked to be taken to the sea. Before the fish swam away, it warned Manu that there would be a huge flood, which would engulf the earth, and it advised the sage to save himself by building a huge boat. Manu did as the fish advised, taking on board the boat all kinds of creatures and seeds of plants.

Almost before he had finished his task, the rains began to fall heavily and soon the whole world was flooded. The waters grew rough and threatened to capsize Manu's craft. However, Matsya appeared again, this time as a gigantic fish, and towed the boat safely through the waters. The fish then told Manu to fasten the boat to the summit of a mountain, which still remained above the water, and to wait for the floods to subside. Before leaving, the fish confessed to Manu that he was in fact Vishnu.

In gratitude to the god, Manu made a sacrifice of milk and melted butter. After a year, the offering turned into a beautiful woman who revealed that she was his daughter, Ida. The couple proceeded to engender the human race.

MANJUSHRI, seated on a lotus-moon throne, wields his sword of wisdom, poised to strike down ignorance.

nobody saw Maitreya because their vision was so clouded. Maitreya then took Asanga to the Tushita heaven, where he was able to gain the spiritual insight which he had sought for so many years.

MANJUSHRI is the BOD-HISATTVA of wisdom and one of the most important members of the Buddhist pantheon. His name means "He Who is Noble and Gentle", and his SHAKTI, or female energy, is SARASVATI. Manjushri is usually depicted with two lotus

blossoms, on which rest his attributes, a sword of wisdom and a sacred text. He dispels ignorance, bestows eloquence and is a symbol of the enlightenment that can be reached through learning. He is said to be the father and mother of the bodhisattvas, as well as their spiritual friend.

In Tibetan Buddhism, certain great saints and scholars are regarded as incarnations of Manjushri. The Tibetans often depict Manjushri with several heads and arms. In Nepal, he is believed to have introduced civilized life, and his festival is celebrated on the first day of the year. According to legend, Manjushri originally came from China. In Japan he is known as Monju-Bosatzu. (See also BOD-HISATTVAS)

MANU, according to Hindu mythology, was the first man and the precursor of humankind. One myth tells how Manu was the son of BRAHMA and a young woman whom the god had produced from his own body. According to

MARA is the evil demon of Buddhist belief who tempted *GAUTAMA BUDDHA* as he sat meditating under the sacred tree at Bodh Gaya. Mara's name means "Death". He realized that if Gautama achieved enlightenment, his own power would be destroyed, and he therefore sent his three beautiful daughters to tempt the sage. Although Mara's daughters sang and danced and tried every trick they knew to beguile him, Gautama remained unmoved. Eventually, they admitted defeat.

Mara then sent an army of terrifying devils to threaten Gautama. Some of the creatures had 1,000 eyes, others were horrifically deformed; they drank blood and ate snakes. However, as soon as they came near to the sacred tree, they found that their arms were bound to their sides. Finally, Mara himself attacked Gautama with his fearsome weapon, a disc which could slice mountains in two. None the less, when the disc

MARA (below) sent his three beautiful daughters to tempt Gautama and tried in every way to threaten the sage as he sat meditating under the sacred tree at Bodh Gaya. (TIBETAN PAINTING, 18TH CENTURY.)

MAYA (above) gave birth to Gautama Buddha while holding on to the branch of a tree. He is also shown taking seven symbolic steps. (TIBETAN PAINTING, 18TH CENTURY.)

reached Gautama, it was transformed into a garland of flowers. At last, the demon realized that he was beaten.

THE MARUTS are a group of either 27 or 60 storm gods, usually said to be the sons of the goddess Prisni and *RUDRA*, an ancient Vedic deity who later came to be identified with *SHIVA*. The Maruts accompanied the war god *INDRA* and were armed with lightning arrows and thunderbolts. According to the *Rig Veda*, the ancient collection of sacred hymns, they wore golden helmets and breastplates, and used their axes to split the clouds so that rain could fall. They were widely regarded as clouds, capable of shaking mountains and destroying forests.

According to a later tradition, the Maruts were born from the broken womb of the goddess Diti, after Indra hurled a thunderbolt at her to prevent her from giving birth to too powerful a son. The goddess

had intended to remain pregnant for a century before giving birth to a son who would threaten Indra.

MATSYA see *MANU*.

MAYA, or Queen Mahamaya, was the mother of *GAUTAMA BUDDHA*. According to Buddhist tradition, she possessed all the qualities required of a woman destined to bear a buddha. She was not passionate, she drank no alcohol and she observed the precepts of a lay Buddhist. On the day she conceived Gautama, she is said to have had a dream in which a small white elephant, carrying a white lotus in its trunk, entered her right side. In due course, Maya gave birth to Gautama from her side as she stood holding on to a tree. She suffered no pain. Seven days later, she died of joy and joined the gods.

Maya, or "Miraculous Power", was a term used in Hinduism to describe the power of the Vedic gods. Later, Maya was regarded as the illusion of reality which we perceive, which will be dispelled when the universal reality of Brahman or the "Absolute" is understood. (See also *THE LIFE OF THE BUDDHA*)

MAYA (above) dreams of a small white elephant and conceives Gautama Buddha, who is seen arriving for reincarnation, riding on the elephant.

MERU is a mythical world mountain, also known as Sumeru. According to ancient Indian beliefs, both Buddhist and Hindu, it is situated at the centre of the universe and is the dwelling place of the gods. In Hindu tradition, the sacred Ganges flows from the summit of Mount Meru, and BRAHMA's magnificent golden city is situated at its peak. Beneath the mountain lie seven lower worlds, in the lowest of which lives the snake Vasuki, who bears Mount Meru and all the worlds on his coils and destroys them at the end of each YUGA.

In Buddhist belief, Meru is surrounded by seas and worlds, beneath which lie the hells. The realms of the gods and the Buddha-fields are situated above the mountain. According to one Tibetan myth, in the very beginning, there was nothing but emptiness. Eventually, a wind began to stir, caused by the karma of the inhabitants of a previous universe. After many ages, the winds grew stronger, and rain began to fall. Many years later, the primeval or cosmic ocean arose, and the winds began to move the waters of the ocean, churning them until they gave rise to the cosmic mountain Meru, or Rirap Lhunpo. In due course, Meru became the abode of the gods and semi-divine beings.

Meru is made of precious stones; its slopes are covered with trees and fruits. Around the mountain lies a vast lake, and around the lake lies a ring of golden mountains. Altogether, there are seven rings of mountains and seven lakes. The final lake is Chi Gyatso, within which lie the four worlds. Each world is like an island and has its own unique inhabitants. Our own world is called Czambu Ling. At first, Czambu Ling was inhabited by gods from Mount Meru. Everyone was happy, there was no illness or pain.

However, it so happened that one day, one of the gods noticed a creamy substance lying on the sur-

MERU (right), the golden mountain, is the centre of the world in both Hindu and Buddhist mythology. (MURAL PAINTING, WAT KO KEO SUTTHARAM, THAILAND.)

face of the earth. The cream tasted delicious, and soon all the other gods began to eat it. The more the gods ate, the less powerful they became. Eventually, the light the gods had radiated was extinguished, the world became dark and the gods became human beings. When the creamy food ran out, the people began to eat fruit. Each individual had his own plant, and each day the plant would produce just one piece of fruit, which was just enough to satisfy one person's hunger.

One day, a man noticed that his plant had produced two pieces of fruit. He ate both pieces and, when the next day his plant produced no fruit, he stole some from his neighbour's plant. In this way, theft and greed were introduced to the world. (See also MYTHICAL MOUNTAINS)

MGON-PO see MAHAKALA.

MITRA, according to Vedic mythology, was a god of light. He was one of the ADITYAS, and was closely associated with VARUNA, the supreme Vedic deity. Sometimes regarded as twins, Mitra and Varuna maintained universal order and justice and were said to embody the power that formed the essence of the kshatriya, or warrior caste. A good-natured deity, Mitra has particular responsibility for friendships and contracts. He is believed to direct human beings towards the light and to enable them to live happily with one another. In Iran, his parallel is the god Mithra.

MURUKAN, or the "Youthful One", was a deity of the Dravidians of southern India. He is sometimes known as Ceyon, or the "Red One". He is an important figure in present-day Tamil religion. Murukan is usually represented riding an elephant or a peacock, and he carries a spear and a garland of flowers. He is sometimes identified with KARTTIKEYA, the Hindu warrior god. His equivalent in Sri Lanka is KATARAGAMA DEVIYO.

SACRED RIVERS

THE GREAT RIVER GANGES, which rises in the Himalayas and flows across north-east India, is sacred to Hindus, who believe that bathing in her water will enable them to reach Indra's heaven, Svarga, on Mount Meru. They also revere the holy city of Prayaga (now Allahabad), where the Ganges is joined by her two tributaries, the Yamuna and the subterranean Sarasvati. This is a place of pilgrimage so sacred that a tiny piece of its soil is believed to be capable of wiping away sin. Each of these great rivers was deified as a goddess, of which the most holy was Ganga, daughter of the mountain god Himavat and an aspect of the great mother goddess, Devi. She was said to have emerged from the toe of Vishnu, and to have descended from heaven to cleanse the earth of the accumulated ashes of the dead. The ashes of the faithful are still committed to her care.

SARASVATI (above), the goddess, was originally identified with the sacred river which flows into the Ganges at Prayaga. As the deity of a natural force, she had the power to smash mountains and spoke with the roar of the waterfall. Later, she was said to be the creation and consort of Brahma. She became the goddess of music and wisdom, was credited with the invention of Sanskrit, and was known as the "Mother of the Veda". (MARBLE STATUE, 12TH CENTURY.)

VARANASI (left), the city on the west bank of the Ganges, is a holy place for Hindus. They believe that to die here, or to have their ashes committed to the river, will release their souls from the cycle of rebirth and death. The dead are cremated on the "burning" ghats (the stone steps that run down to the water), and their ashes are given to the Ganges to be carried down to the sea.

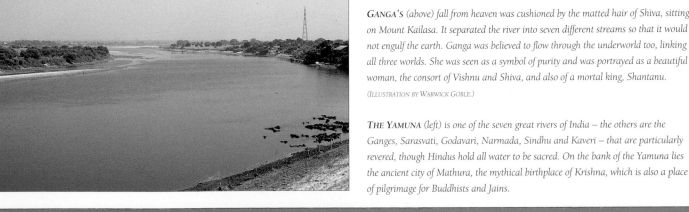

YAMUNA (left), the river goddess, was the daughter of the sun god Surya and his wife Sanjna, and was also sometimes said to be the sister of Yama, the Vedic god of death. As a river goddess, she was thought to bring fertility and good harvests, and was therefore identified with prosperity. The river Yamuna, a tributary of the Ganges, parted miraculously to allow Krishna's father, Vasudev, to carry him to safety as a baby. (STONE CARVING, 9TH CENTURY.)

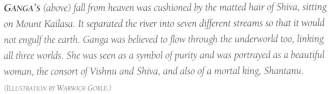

GANGA'S (above) fall from heaven was cushioned by the matted hair of Shiva, sitting on Mount Kailasa. It separated the river into seven different streams so that it would not engulf the earth. Ganga was believed to flow through the underworld too, linking all three worlds. She was seen as a symbol of purity and was portrayed as a beautiful woman, the consort of Vishnu and Shiva, and also of a mortal king, Shantanu. (ILLUSTRATION BY WARWICK GOBLE.)

THE YAMUNA (left) is one of the seven great rivers of India – the others are the Ganges, Sarasvati, Godavari, Narmada, Sindhu and Kaveri – that are particularly revered, though Hindus hold all water to be sacred. On the bank of the Yamuna lies the ancient city of Mathura, the mythical birthplace of Krishna, which is also a place of pilgrimage for Buddhists and Jains.

P

NAGAS, according to Hindu belief, are semi-divine but powerful serpents who guard the treasures of the earth. They are often associated with fertility but can occasionally prove dangerous. Whereas some nagas are depicted with several heads, others are represented as human beings. The naga Vasuki was used as a rope in the myth of the churning of the ocean and was afterwards worn by *SHIVA* as a girdle that had the power to dispel demons. When the great god *VISHNU* is resting, he sleeps on the naga known as Sesha, or Ananta. Seshas's hoods shade the god, but his yawns cause earthquakes.

In Buddhist belief, the nagas are often regarded as water deities who guard Buddhist texts. One story tells how the nagas took the Buddhist philosopher Nagarjuna to their realm, where he rediscovered the *Prajnaparamita-sutra* of Mahayana Buddhism. The *GAUTAMA BUDDHA* is said to have given the text to the nagas for safekeeping until a time when humans were ready to receive it. Another story tells how the naga king Elapatra disguised himself as a man to listen to the Buddha preach.

Naga kings are depicted in representations of Gautama Buddha's birth. One such king, Mucilinda, is said to have sheltered the meditating Buddha during a great storm by surrounding him with the coils of his body and forming an awning

NAGAS are semi-divine but powerful serpents who guard the treasures of the earth. (ALAMPUR, 7TH–8TH CENTURY.)

with his hood. The naga kings are said to control rainfall and to look after rivers, lakes and seas. They protect against fires caused by lightning. In spring, the nagas climb to the heavens, whereas in winter they live deep in the earth.

NANDA see *KRISHNA*.

NANDI, or Nandin, is the milk-white bull who is an animal form of *SHIVA*, the great Hindu god. As well

as being Shiva's chosen mount, Nandi is a member of his retinue and represents the great god's virility and fertility.

When Shiva took the form of Nataraja, Nandi provided the music for his wild dancing. In the *Puranas*, Hindu scriptures dating from the fifth century AD, Nandi is invoked as a divinity. He is the son of Surabhi, the divine cow who arose from the churning of the ocean, and *KASYAPA*, the sage.

Nandi looks after all four-legged creatures and stands guard at the four corners of the world. A sculpture of the bull is usually situated at the entrance of temples dedicated to Shiva.

NANDIN see *NANDI*.

NANG-LHA is one of the supernatural beings of the indigenous Bon religion of Tibet. He was assimilated into the Buddhist pantheon as a protector of the religion.

NANDI's statue stands at the entrance of many temples dedicated to Shiva, and devotees customarily touch the bull's testicles as they enter the shrine. Nandi is Shiva's principal attendant.

Nang-Lha looks after the house and is usually shown with the head of a pig and the body of a human being.

NARASIMHA was the fourth incarnation, or *AVATAR*, of the great Hindu god *VISHNU*, preserver of the universe. A man-lion, he overcame the king Hiranyakashipu, an incarnation of *RAVANA*. See also *THE AVATARS OF VISHNU*)

NARAYANA see *BRAHMA*.

NASATYA see *ASVINS*.

NATARAJA see *SHIVA*.

NATHA is one of the four principal gods of Sri Lanka. His name means "Master". He was identified with the *BODHISATTVA*, or "buddha-to-be", *AVALOKITESHVARA*, and was also sometimes regarded as *MAITREYA*, the future Buddha. The Buddhist goddess *TARA* is said to be his consort.

NILARANTHA see *SHIVA*.

PADMASAMBHAVA was one of the founders of Tibetan Buddhism. His followers worship him as the

NARASIMHA was a man-lion, the fourth avatar of the Hindu god Vishnu. He overcame the demon king Hiranyakashipu. (CARVING, HALEBIDU, KARNATAKA.)

"second Buddha". A contemporary of the Tibetan king Trisong Detsen (AD 755–97), Padmasambhava was allegedly born in the mythical land of Urgyen, believed to be situated in north-west Kashmir. He is said to have been created by the buddha *AMITABHA* and to have appeared, aged eight years old, in a lotus blossom, thereby earning his name, which means "He Who is Born from the Lotus".

After murdering a king's minister, Padmasambhava was condemned to live in the charnel grounds. However, while there, he mastered all the learned disciplines of his time, in particular the teachings of the Tantras, and achieved great spiritual power through conversing with the *DAKINI*, the female "Sky-goers". At that time, the ancient Bon religion still flourished in Tibet. King Trisong Detsen decided that he wanted to intro-

duce Buddhism to the country, and so sent messengers to India, instructing them to find the most learned men in order that they might teach his people. The messengers advised the king to send for Padmasambhava.

Padmasambhava arrived in Tibet and imparted the Buddhist teachings to 25 main students, as well as to the king. Some accounts say that he stayed for a few months, others that he was in Tibet for 50 years. He transformed many demons into *DHARMAPALAS*, or "Protectors of the Teaching", founded the "Inconceivable" temple with the help of local spirits, and composed the "Hidden Treasures". The treasures, known as Gter-ma, are religious instructions, which are said to have been hidden away in order to be revealed sometime in the future when the world needs a fresh revelation.

PADMASAMBHAVA was worshipped as the "second Buddha" and instrumental in introducing Buddhism to Tibet. (PAINTING, TANKA LAMA SCHOOL, 19TH CENTURY.)

One story tells how the king eventually grew worried that his people showed greater reverence for Padmasambhava than for himself. In order to demonstrate his supreme authority, he summoned all his courtiers to watch Padmasambhava bow down before him. However, as Padmasambhava raised his arms as if to prostrate himself before the king, flames sprang from his fingertips, setting the ruler's clothes on fire. Immediately, the king tore off his ceremonial scarf, already smouldering, and threw himself at Padmasambhava's feet in submission. He later gave Padmasambhava the scarf as a token of his humility, establishing the tradition of giving scarves as a sign of respect.

Before leaving Tibet, the sage promised to return every month on the tenth day of the waxing moon in order to bless anyone who called out his name. According to legend, he travelled to Bhutan, where he

PADMASAMBHAVA in his eight forms. He built the first Tibetan Buddhist monastery, at Samyé, where previous attempts had been foiled by demons, who tore down the buildings as soon as they were erected.

continued his religious teaching. Padmasambhava is said to have lived for more than 1,000 years.

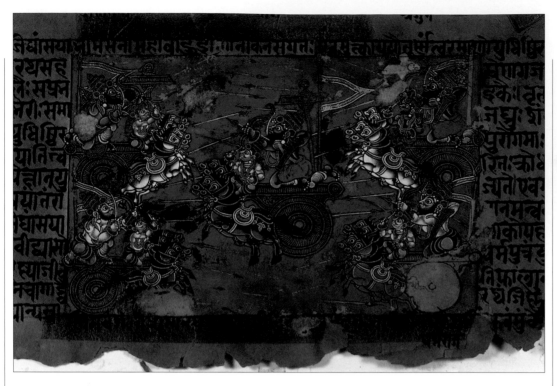

THE PANDAVAS *were descended from King Pandu. Two of their number, Bhima and Arjuna, fought against Drona, the leader of the Kauravas. (ILLUSTRATION TO THE MAHABHARATA, INDIA, C. 1542.)*

THE PANDAVAS

THE PANDAVAS were the descendants of King Pandu. The five Pandava princes fought the Kauravas in the famous battle of Kurukshetra, which is described in the Hindu epic, the *Mahabharata*.

On the eve of the battle, *ARJUNA*, one of the five brothers, received spiritual instruction from *KRISHNA*, an *AVATAR* of the great god *VISHNU*, who disguised himself as Arjuna's charioteer. Krishna's teaching forms the *Bhagavad Gita* or "Song of the Lord".

PARASHURAMA see *AVATARS*.

PARVATI is an aspect of the divine mother of Hindu mythology, the consort of the great god *SHIVA*. She is the graceful aspect of the *SHAKTI* of Shiva. Parvati's name means "Daughter of the Mountains"; her father was Himavat, king of the mountains, and she was the mother of the elephant god *GANESHA*, whom she is sometimes said to have created from the rubbings of her own body. According to one myth, Shiva produced six

PARVATI (right), mother of the elephant-headed god Ganesha, with Shiva, who is shown with the goddess Ganga in his hair. (ILLUSTRATION BY J. HIGGINBOTHAM, 1864.)

children without Parvati's assistance. The goddess became extremely fond of her husband's offspring and one day hugged them so tightly that they merged into one child, although the six heads remained. The boy grew up to become the warrior god *KARTTIKEYA*, or Skanda. According to another story, when Parvati first saw Karttikeya, she felt such maternal love for him that milk flowed from her breasts.

Another tale tells how Shiva criticized Parvati's dark skin, whereupon the goddess retired to the forest in shame and became an ascetic. However, *BRAHMA* was so impressed by Parvati's austerities that he transformed her into Gauri, the golden-skinned goddess. In some versions of the story, Parvati's dark skin became the goddess *KALI*.

Shiva once turned Parvati into a fisherwoman to punish her disobedience. On another occasion, Parvati crept up behind Shiva and put her fingers over his eyes. Darkness enveloped the world, and so Shiva made a third eye appear in the middle of his forehead. (See also *MYTHICAL MOUNTAINS*; *THE MOTHER GODDESS*)

PATTINI is the most important Singhalese goddess. She is said to look after marriages and to keep epidemics at bay. According to one myth, she was born from a mango, which had been struck by a divine arrow. Another myth tells how she introduced the cultivation of rice into Sri Lanka.

THE PEY, according to the Tamils of southern India and Sri Lanka, are demons who drink the blood of the dead and of wounded warriors, and bring misery and bad luck to the living. They are wild creatures with tangled hair.

PRADYUMNA, according to Hindu mythology, was the son of *KRISHNA*, the eighth *AVATAR* of *VISHNU*, and his wife Rukmuni. He is sometimes said to have been a reincarnation of *KAMA*, god of desire. When he was six days old, Pradyumna was kidnapped by a demon, Shambhara, who threw him into the sea. The infant was swallowed by a fish, which was later caught and brought to Shambhara's home. Pradyumna

PARVATI with her husband, Shiva, and children Karttikeya and Ganesha, in their home on Mount Kailasa, attended by Nandi, the bull. (MINIATURE, 18TH CENTURY.)

Prajapati then created night and day, the seasons, death, and people to relieve his loneliness.

The name Prajapati sometimes refers to a variety of gods, including *INDRA, SOMA, SHIVA, GARUDA, KRISHNA* and *MANU*. It is also the name given to ten sages from whom humanity is said to be descended, and to seven *RISHIS*, or seers. *BRAHMA* is sometimes attributed with myths that later became associated with Prajapati.

PRAJNA see *HERUKA.*

PRAJNAPARAMITA, according to Buddhist belief, is the deification of the *Prajnaparamita-sutra*, a sacred text in which *GAUTAMA BUDDHA* is said to have set out his teachings. According to tradition, the Buddha gave the text to the *NAGAS* until the time was ripe for it to be revealed to the faithful. The sutra is said to have been "restored" by the Buddhist philosopher Nagarjuna.

Prajnaparamita is thus regarded as an incarnation of the divine word. Her name means "Perfection of Insight" or "Wisdom that Reaches the Other Shore". In Tibet, the goddess is usually depicted coloured white or yellow, holding a lotus flower in one hand and the sacred text in the other.

emerged from the fish, and Mayadevi, the mistress of the house, looked after him. The sage Narada, lord of the *GANDHARVAS*, told her who the child was. When Pradyumna became a young man, Mayadevi fell in love with him and told him the truth about his origins. Pradyumna then killed Shambhara and fled with Mayadevi to Krishna's palace.

PRAHLADA see *AVATARS.*

PRAJAPATI, according to Hindu mythology, is the lord or master of created beings. In the Hindu epic, the *Mahabharata*, he is the protector of the sexual organ. By his own powers, he produced numerous children including a daughter, *USHAS*, or "Dawn".

On one occasion, Prajapati attempted to commit incest with Ushas, whereupon she transformed herself into a gazelle or deer. Prajapati then took the form of a stag, whose seed gave rise to the first humans. In other versions of the myth, Prajapati succeeded in mating with Ushas when she appeared in numerous different animal forms. The couple thereby gave rise to all living creatures. Another myth tells how Prajapati rose weeping from the primordial waters. The tears that fell into the water became the earth, whereas those that the god wiped away became the sky and the air.

PRITHIVI, a Vedic earth goddess, is sometimes said to be the mother of *USHAS*, the dawn, *AGNI*, the god of fire, and *INDRA*, the great war god. She is also the consort of Dyaus, the sky father of the Vedic religion. When giving birth to Indra, numerous portents warned the goddess that this particular son was destined to supplant the old order. As a result, she hid the child away. Prithivi is usually depicted in the form of a cow.

R

PURURAVAS see *APSARAS*.

PURUSHA was the primordial man or cosmic giant of Indian mythology. According to the ancient sacred hymns known as the *Rig Veda*, Purusha was three-quarters immortal and one-quarter mortal. From his mortal quarter, he released his wife, Viraj, and he was then born from her as a universal spirit. Purusha assumed the form of a giant with 1,000 thighs, 1,000 feet, 1,000 arms, 1,000 eyes, 1,000 faces and 1,000 heads.

In order that the world might be created, he offered himself up to be sacrificed. His head became the heavens, his navel, the atmosphere and his feet, the earth. The seasons came from his armpits, the earth from his feet, the sun from his eyes, and the moon from his mind. The gods and people of the brahman caste came from his mouth, and the wind was born from his breath. His arms became the kshatriyas, or warrior caste; his thighs became the vaishyas, or the traders and farmers; and his feet became the shudras, or servant class.

In the *Brahmanas* and the *Upanishads*, religious texts composed after the *Rig Veda*, Purusha was regarded as *PRAJAPATI*, the lord of created beings. His name is also used to denote the spiritual core of a person; in Buddhist texts, it is sometimes applied to the Buddha.

RADHA (above) and Krishna walking by the Yamuna river in the moonlight, having exchanged clothes. (ILLUSTRATION TO THE BHAGAVATA PURANA, KANGRA, C. 1820.)

PURUSHA (left) was the primal being of Indian mythology. He was sacrificed to create all living things.

RADHA, according to Hindu mythology, was the favourite gopi, or cowgirl, of *KRISHNA*, the eighth *AVATAR* of the great god *VISHNU*. She lived in Vrindavan, the village in northern India where Krishna was brought up. Radha is sometimes regarded as Krishna's wife, sometimes as his lover. According to one tale, she was married to Ayanagosha, a cowherd. When Ayanagosha heard of Radha's adultery, he went in search of the couple. However, Krishna assumed the form of a goddess, and they thereby escaped Ayanagosha's

asleep with Rahula in her arms, feared he might wake them and so left them sleeping.

Rahula entered a Buddhist community at the age of seven and is regarded as the guardian of novices. He is one of the ten great disciples of the Buddha and was said to be "first in esoteric practices and in desire for instruction in the Law". He died before the Buddha. He is sometimes represented holding a fly whisk (swatter) and a scroll of scriptures, and is often accompanied by a deer or a disciple.

RAKSHASAS, according to Hindu belief, are semi-divine, usually evil-natured, spirits. They are able to assume any shape they choose. Whereas they tend to be good-natured and faithful towards one another, with outsiders they can be gluttonous, lustful and violent. They live in a magnificent city, designed by Vishvakarma, the architect of the gods. Harmless beings, such as the YAKSHAS, are rakshasas, as are numerous enemies of the gods, including demons who live in cemeteries and harass human beings.

According to one tradition, the rakshasas emerged from BRAHMA's foot, whereas another tradition tells how they are descendants of KASYAPA, the great RISHI, or sage. In some texts, the rakshasas are described as the original inhabitants of India who were subjugated by the Aryans.

wrath. According to another tradition, Radha is an incarnation of LAKSHMI, the goddess of good fortune and wife of Vishnu. The goddess took the form of Radha in order that she might not be separated from her husband.

Radha's love for Krishna is seen as a symbol of the interplay between the individual soul and the divine. When Radha is apart from Krishna, she longs for his return, and Krishna likewise pines for Radha. Devotees of Krishna regard the human feeling of love and surrender as a means of achieving knowledge of and union with the divine.

RAHU see AMRITA.

RAHULA, whose name means "Fetter", was the son of GAUTAMA BUDDHA and the princess Yasodhara. He is usually said to have been born shortly before Gautama left his family to seek enlightenment, although he is sometimes said to have been born on the day of his father's enlightenment. According to the former version of the myth, Gautama crept into his wife's rooms to kiss her goodbye but, seeing her

RADHA (right) listens to her lover, Krishna, (left), entertaining her with his flute as she attends to her toilette.

(MINIATURE, 18TH CENTURY.)

THE MOTHER GODDESS

DEVI, OR MAHADEVI ("THE GREAT GODDESS"), is a composite figure who includes various aspects of the female deity in a series of contrasting incarnations. In the earliest Indian cultures, the mother goddess was Shakti, the source of all energy in the universe, the creative force who brought fertility to the earth. Some of her manifestations were associated with natural forces, such as Ushas, the dawn, and Ganga, the river. Later she was subsumed in the patriarchal Hindu creation myth as the consort of Shiva. In this role she continued to appear in a variety of incarnations. Some were benign, such as Sati and Parvati, both of whom were loving and caring, but others were terrifying, such as the warrior goddesses Durga and Kali. Although she lost her autonomy in her new role as consort, she was still the creative force. While Shiva embodied potency, Shakti was the energy needed to release his power.

KALI (above), the "Black One", was the most terrifying aspect of the goddess Devi. She was portrayed as a black-skinned hag with pendulous breasts and a necklace of skulls or severed heads. Like Shiva, she had an all-seeing third eye in her forehead. Her male victims, made impotent without the goddess's activating energy, had no way of resisting her attack. (THE GODDESS BEHEADING A MAN, BUNDI, C. 1650.)

UMA (right) was an early form of the goddess Parvati, the shakti of Shiva. Uma was the consort of Chandrashekhara, an aspect of Shiva who was also called Umapati ("Uma's spouse"). She was the daughter of Himavat, the king of the Himalayas. In her fierce aspect as Uma Maheshvara, she fought with demons. (KHMER STATUE, 11TH CENTURY.)

PARVATI (above right), the wife of Shiva (above left), was a reincarnation of his first wife, Sati, who had immolated herself in shame when Shiva was not invited to her father Daksha's sacrifice. Shiva showed no interest in Parvati at first, objecting to her dark skin, but she won his love by enduring austerities. She became the personification of the loving wife and mother, domesticating Shiva, and they led an idyllic family life with their children Karttikeya (above centre) and Ganesha. (BRONZE SOMASKANDA GROUP, 16TH CENTURY.)

DURGA (left) the invincible warrior goddess, fought demons that threatened the world. She was the embodiment of the anger of the gods, whether of Shiva and Vishnu, or of Parvati. When Durga herself was angry, Kali emerged from her forehead. Durga fought the demon Mahisha in an epic battle, in which he transformed himself into a buffalo, a lion, an armed man and an elephant. Finally, Durga cut off Mahisha's head. (DURGA SLAYS MAHISHASURA, MANDI, C. 1750–60.)

KALI (right) set out to kill demons but could become so intoxicated with blood that she threatened the world as well. She vanquished the demon Raktabija, who was reproduced with every drop of his blood that touched the ground, by catching the drops in her huge mouth before they fell, and then sucking the demon dry. Inflamed by her feast, she began to dance wildly, and when Shiva tried to stop her, she danced on his body, nearly destroying the cosmos. (ILLUSTRATION BY J. HIGGINBOTHAM, 1864.)

RAMA (above) and his brothers getting married. Rama was married to Sita, regarded by devotees of Vishnu as the ideal woman. (KULU-MANDI, PAHARI SCHOOL, 1760–65.)

RAMA (left) and his half-brother, Lakshmana left Sita alone to hunt a golden deer planted in the forest by Ravana. Meanwhile, the demon captured Sita. (MUGHAL PAINTING, EARLY 17TH CENTURY.)

RAMA was an *AVATAR*, or incarnation, of *VISHNU*, the great Hindu deity known as the preserver of the universe. He is said to have been sent down to earth in order to overcome the powers of darkness as embodied by the evil demon *RAVANA*, king of *LANKA*. His life and exploits are immortalized in the Hindu epic, the *Ramayana*.

Rama probably originated as a folk hero and only gradually came to be regarded as an avatar of Vishnu. He was courageous and peace-loving, dutiful and virtuous. Devotees of Vishnu regard him as the ideal man and they regard his wife, *SITA*, as the ideal woman: chaste, faithful and devout.

Rama was said to be the son of King Dasaratha of Ayodhya. On his father's death, his stepmother Sumitra cheated him out of his inheritance and banished him into exile in the forest for 14 years. Although Rama advised his wife to stay in the palace, away from the hardships of forest life, Sita insisted on accompanying her husband: "With you it is heaven, away from you hell," she said. Once in the forest, Rama protected the sages who had their hermitages there. When Rama failed to respond to the advances of a horrible female demon, Surpanaka, she persuaded her brother, Ravana, to kidnap Sita. Ravana succeeded in abducting Sita and carried her off to the island of Lanka. Rama, mad with grief, went in search of his wife and succeeded in overcoming numerous demons, often with the help of the monkey god *HANUMAN*.

In order to reach Sita, Rama had to take his army across the sea. He asked the ocean for help and, when none was forthcoming, became so enraged that he shot his arrows at the waters in an attempt to dry them up. Nothing happened. Rama then fired an arrow tipped with a charm given to him by *BRAHMA*. Immediately, the sky grew dark, and all living creatures trembled with fear. Finally, the ocean spoke and explained that, though he was unable to halt the movements of his waters, he would support a bridge over which Rama's soldiers could cross. Soon, Hanuman's army of monkeys had built a bridge and the troops began to cross over to Lanka. Immediately, Rama and Ravana entered into a fearsome battle. Rama's army appeared to be winning when Ravana approached to attack Rama in person. Rama destroyed the demon's ten heads one after another, but new ones kept growing in their place. Finally, Rama fired an arrow which the sage *AGASTYA* had given to him. The arrow killed Ravana, then returned to Rama. The battle was won.

Despite Sita's innocence, she repulsed Rama, since her reputation had been stained by her long stay with Ravana. Sita despaired and threw herself on to a funeral pyre. *AGNI*, the fire god, rescued her from the flames. In another version of the story, Sita remained unharmed by the flames, thus publicly proving her innocence.

Rama regained his kingdom and ruled over it with wisdom, fairness and tenderness for 1,000 years. He finally returned to heaven where he was reunited with Vishnu. The

RAMA (far left) spurned the advances of the sister of the demon Ravana. In revenge, she persuaded Ravana to kidnap Rama's wife Sita. (ILLUSTRATION BY WARWICK GOBLE.)

RAMA (left) gives his ring to Hanuman for the monkey god to send to Sita. Hanuman is the courageous and ever-loyal supporter of Rama. (ILLUSTRATION BY WARWICK GOBLE.)

victory of Rama over Ravana continues to be celebrated annually in India at the festival of Dussehra. In northern India, his name refers to the supreme god. His attributes are a bow and arrows. (See also *THE AVATARS OF VISHNU*)

RATI see *KAMA*.

RATNASAMBHAVA is one of the *DHYANIBUDDHAS*, "Great Buddhas of Wisdom". He is the "Source of Secret Things" and "He Who is Born of the Jewel". In Tibet he is often shown embracing Mamaki, his *SHAKTI*. His element is fire, his heavenly quarter the south, and he is yellow in colour. His carriage is drawn by a pair of lions or a horse.

RAVANA was the demon king of *LANKA* whom *RAMA*, an *AVATAR* of the great god *VISHNU*, was sent down to earth to vanquish. He had ten heads and was said to be indestructible. In the Hindu epic, the *Ramayana*, he is portrayed as the embodiment of evil. According to one tradition, a high-ranking member of Vishnu's heaven committed a sin and was given the choice of two means to clear his name: he could either descend to earth and live out seven incarnations as a friend of Vishnu or three incarnations as the enemy of the god. The offender chose the latter option, believing that he would thereby return to heaven more quickly.

Ravana's first incarnation was as the demon king Hiranyakashipu. Such was his power that he

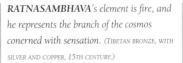

RATNASAMBHAVA's element is fire, and he represents the branch of the cosmos conerned with sensation. (TIBETAN BRONZE, WITH SILVER AND COPPER, 15TH CENTURY.)

dethroned the mighty god *INDRA* and shut the gods out of heaven. He proclaimed himself king of the universe and ordered everyone to worship him. However, his son Prahlada persisted in worshipping Vishnu; try as he might, the demon king was unable to sway him from his vocation. Hiranyakashipu determined to kill Prahlada, but Vishnu protected him. Eventually, Vishnu destroyed the demon and Prahlada became king.

Ravana's second incarnation was as the enemy of Rama, another avatar of Vishnu. Ravana abducted Vishnu's wife, *SITA*, and took her away to the island of Lanka. Helped by the monkey god *HANUMAN*, Rama found her there and made war against the demon, eventually killing him. On the eve of the great battle in which he was slain, the demon admitted that he had only kidnapped Sita in order that he might be killed and so go on to live out his third incarnation as a demon, after which he would be able to return to heaven.

In his third incarnation, Ravana appeared as the demon Sisupala. The son of a king, he had three eyes

and four arms. Although his parents were horrified at the sight of him, they were reassured by a voice which told them that, until the time of his death, Sisupala would be both famous and fortunate. The voice also announced that his mother would be able to recognize whoever it was that would eventually kill the boy: when the child sat on his knee, his third eye and extra arms would disappear.

The king and queen travelled from kingdom to kingdom, placing their son on the knee of each ruler, but nothing happened. When they returned home the young prince *KRISHNA*, the eighth avatar of Vishnu, visited the palace. As soon as Sisupala sat on Krishna's knee, his third eye vanished, and his extra two arms fell off. The queen then begged Krishna to forgive her child should he ever offend him. Krishna agreed that he would.

Years later, Sisupala attended a great sacrifice along with numerous important kings. Krishna was also present. The celebration was hosted by King Yudhishthira, who decided that the first homage should be paid to Krishna. Sisupala was outraged, saying that many of the guests present were more important than Krishna. Sisupala appealed to *BRAHMA* for advice, who simply said that Krishna himself should settle the dispute. Sisupala was furious and insulted Brahma, who proceeded to tell the guests the story of Sisupala and the predictions made about him at his birth. Sisupala became increasingly angry and, drawing his sword, continued to insult Brahma. Krishna's flaming disc then rose into the air, shot towards Sisupala and cut him in two. Sisupala's soul appeared as leaping fire and, moving towards Krishna, was absorbed into the hero's feet.

RAVANA (above left), the demon king of Lanka, is conquered by Rama, who rides away in triumph with his wife Sita.

RAVANA (above right) with Hanuman, the monkey god. When Ravana abducted Rama's wife Sita, Hanuman leapt across

the waters to the island of Lanka to discover where Ravana had hidden her.

(ILLUSTRATIONS BY J. HIGGINBOTHAM, 1864.)

S

RIRAP LHUNPO see *MERU*.

RISHIS are usually regarded as the seers and great sages of Hinduism, but the term is also applied to saints and inspired poets. The Veda, the sacred knowledge of the Hindus, was said to have been revealed to the seven great rishis who preserved and transmitted it. The identity of these seven great rishis varies. According to the *Shatapatha Brahmana*, a commentary on the Veda, they were *GAUTAMA*, Bharadvaja, Vishvamitra, Janmadagni, Vasishtha, *KASYAPA* and Atri. The seven great rishis were sometimes regarded as holy beings who were identified with the seven stars of the Great Bear.

RUDRA appears in the *Rig Veda*, the great collection of ancient Indian hymns. His name means "Howler" or the "Red One". A god of storms and the dead, he was sometimes associated with the destructive aspect of the fire god *AGNI*. According to one myth, he emerged from the forehead of *BRAHMA* when the god became angry. Rudra fired his arrows of disease at gods, men and animals, but he also brought health and performed good deeds.

When *PRAJAPATI* committed incest with *USHAS*, the dawn, Rudra was about to shoot him when Prajapati promised to make

him lord of animals. In this role, Rudra was represented in the form of a bull. He gradually came to be seen as an increasingly dark god who developed into the destructive aspect of *SHIVA*. He is often regarded as the father of the *MARUTS*, companions of *INDRA*.

THE SA-DAG are the supernatural "Lords of the Soil" of the indigenous Bon religion of Tibet. They were assimilated into the Buddhist pantheon as protectors of the religion and are propitiated before any building work or farming is carried out.

SAMANTABHADRA is an emanation of the *DHYANIBUDDHA VAIROCANA*, and represents the Buddhist law and compassion. He is one of the most important *BODHISATTVAS* of Mahayana, or "Great Vehicle" Buddhism, and is worshipped as the protector of all those

SAMANTABHADRA, enthroned on a lotus, is mounted on his six-tusked white elephant, which also stands on lotus flowers. (EMEI, SICHUAN, CHINA.)

who teach the dharma, or law. Samantabhadra is often depicted together with *GAUTAMA BUDDHA* and *MANJUSHRI*, bodhisattva of wisdom. He is shown riding on a white elephant with six tusks, a symbol of the ability of wisdom to overcome all obstructions to enlightenment, including the six senses.

SAMVARA, or Chakra Samvara, is a god of initiation in Tantrism, a tradition that uses ritual practices as a path to enlightenment. One of the *YIDAMS* or tutelary gods of Tibet, he is depicted with 12 arms and four or five heads. He is associated with the buddha *AKSOBHYA*. In China, he is believed to be incarnated in the chief Tibetan Buddhist priest in Beijing. His *SHAKTI*, or corresponding female energy, is *VAJRAVARAHI*.

SANI see *AIRAVATA*.

SANJNA see *SURYA*.

SARASVATI is one of the three sacred rivers mentioned in the *Rig Veda*, a collection of ancient Hindu hymns. The Sarasvati is believed to

SAMVARA (above) in the posture of Yab-Yum with his shakti, wears a garland of heads and a crown of skulls. (BRASS AND COPPER, KASHMIR, 9TH CENTURY.)

flow underground to join the other two sacred rivers, the Ganges and the Yamuna, at Allahabad, a town in northern India where mass pilgrimages occur each year.

Sarasvati means "Watery"; as the river, she gives fertility and wisdom to the earth. In later times, Sarasvati became the wife and the creation of *BRAHMA*, the creator of the universe.

Sometimes identified with Vak, the goddess of eloquence, Sarasvati was herself the goddess of language, art and learning. She was sometimes called the "Mother of the Veda", the sacred texts of Hinduism, and was also credited with having invented the Sanskrit alphabet. Offerings are made to her by schoolchildren before classes.

Beautiful but temperamental, she was sometimes depicted with four arms and was represented riding on a swan or peacock, or sitting on a lotus. In some branches of

SARASVATI (right) with Brahma.
Sarasvati was the creation and the wife of
Brahma, the creator of the universe. (CHAPRA
ILLUSTRATION, BIHAR, 1802.)

Buddhism, Sarasvati is the goddess
of instruction and a companion of
the *BODHISATTVA MANJUSHRI*. (See
also *SACRED RIVERS*)

SATI see *DAKSHA*.

SESHA see *NAGAS*.

SHAKTI means "Force", "Power"
or "Energy". In Buddhism, shaktis,
who are female, embody the active
energy of the male deities with
whom they are often shown in a
sexual embrace known as Yab-Yum.
The five main shaktis correspond
to the five male *DHYANIBUDDHAS*,
or the "Great Buddhas of
Wisdom": Vajradharisvari corresponds to *VAIROCANA*, Locana
corresponds to *AKSOBHYA*, Mamaki
corresponds to *RATNASAMBHAVA*,
Pandara corresponds to *AMITABHA*
and Tara to *AMOGHASIDDHI*. When
in Yab-Yum, these shaktis may hold
a cup made from a skull.

In Hinduism, Shakti is regarded
as the creative force of *SHIVA* and is
worshipped under many names,
including *PARVATI*, Uma, *DURGA*
and *KALI*. Shaktism is an aspect of
Tantrism. Shaktas worship Shakti

and revere her as the life-force and
the energy that maintains the universe. As a means towards
experiencing the supreme reality,
Shaktas use sexual practices,
including those shown in the
Kamasutra, the manual of erotic
art. However, in some sects, these
practices are meditated upon rather
than actually performed.

SARASVATI, one of the three sacred rivers
mentioned in the Rig Veda, was also a
beautiful but temperamental goddess,
sometimes depicted with four arms and
sitting on a lotus.

SHAKUNTALA see *APSARAS*.

SHAMBHALA, according to
Tibetan Buddhist mythology, is a
mythical kingdom generally said to
lie to the north-east of India,
although it is also believed to be
located in China and at the North
Pole. It is claimed that the saviour
of the world will appear from
Shambhala when war and destruction threaten civilization. The
Kalachakra teachings, a complex
system of meditation, are also said
to have arisen in Shambhala.
According to tradition, a mythical

king Suchandra ruled over
Shambhala and received the
Kalachakra teachings from the
Buddha in his 80th year. The king
wrote the teachings down and
passed them on through six further
kings and 25 "Proclaimers". At the
time of the 25th teacher, Rigden
Pema Karpo, a golden age will
dawn and Shambhala will become
a universal kingdom.

SHENRAB MIWO see
GSHEN-RAB.

SHITALA see *DURGA*.

SHIVA is one of the principal Hindu deities who, together with *VISHNU* and *BRAHMA*, forms the Trimurti, or triad of great gods. He is believed to have developed from *RUDRA*, a minor deity who appears in the *Rig Veda*, the collection of ancient Hindu hymns dating from between 1500 and 900 BC. It seems that the god grew in stature after absorbing some of the characteristics of an ancient fertility god sometimes referred to as "proto-Shiva". Representations of this god, sitting in the position of a yogi and associated with animals and plants, have been ascribed to the Indus Valley culture, which dates from before 1500 BC.

Shiva can be kind and protective, but he is also terrifying and is found in such places as battlefields and cremation grounds. He is often shown decorated with a string of skulls. Although he is a god of creation, he is also the god of time and thus the great destroyer. He is a fertility god, but he is also an ascetic who has conquered his desires and lives on Mount Kailasa in the high Himalayas, deep in the meditation which keeps the world in existence.

Although Shiva brings death, he also conquers death as well as disease and is invoked to cure sickness. He is sometimes depicted as half-male, half-female. The conflicting qualities and attributes found within the god are intended to symbolize a deity within whom all opposites are reconciled. Even Shiva's name, which means "Auspicious", is intended to reconcile and propitiate the dark aspect of his character, which caused him to be known as the "Destroyer".

As Nataraja, Shiva is the "Lord of the Dance", and is often depicted as such. He dances out the creation of the world, but when he grows tired he relapses into inactivity and the universe becomes chaotic. Destruction thus follows the period of creation. One myth about Shiva as Nataraja concerns the 10,000 *RISHIS*, or sages. Shiva

SHIVA, sitting on a lotus throne and ringed by a circle of flames, sustains the world with his meditation. (PAINTING, C. 1890.)

visited the rishis in order to persuade them to become his devotees. The rishis responded by cursing Shiva and, when this had no effect, they sent a fearsome tiger to devour him. The great god simply removed the skin of the tiger with his fingernail and draped it around his neck like a shawl. The rishis then sent a snake to attack Shiva, who merely hung it around his neck as a garland. Finally, the rishis sent an evil dwarf armed with a club to attack the god, but Shiva responded by placing his foot on the dwarf's back and beginning to dance. The rishis watched the performance in wonder. Even the heavens opened so that the gods were able to look down at the astounding dance. Eventually, the rishis were no longer able to resist the dancing Shiva and threw themselves at his feet.

Shiva's principal symbolic representation is the lingam, a phallic shaped stone. One myth tells how the god visited a pine forest where some sages were meditating. The sages, not recognizing Shiva, suspected him of trying to seduce their wives and caused him to lose his phallus. Immediately, the world grew dark, and the sages lost their virility. Eventually, they made offerings to Shiva, and the world returned to normal.

Shiva is often shown with four arms and with a third eye, the eye of inner vision, in the middle of his forehead. He frequently has a serpent as a necklace, one around his waist and others wrapped around his arms. He may also be depicted smeared with ashes as a symbol of his asceticism. His throat is often coloured blue, and he is sometimes

SHIVA, as Nataraja, the "Lord of the Dance", orders the universe with his dance, with one foot on the back of the dwarf who personifies ignorance. (BRONZE, C. AD 846.)

known as Nilakantha, or "Blue Throat", due to the important part he played in the myth of the churning of the ocean.

According to this popular tale, the great snake Vasuki was used as a rope with which to turn Mount Mandara and so churn the seas in order to produce AMRITA, the elixir of immortality. However, the snake became so exhausted that he eventually spewed out venom, which threatened to destroy all existence. Shiva came to the rescue by swallowing the poison, which stained his throat.

Shiva is the father of the elephant god GANESHA and the warrior god KARTTIKEYA. His mount is the bull NANDI. His consort or SHAKTI (female power) is called PARVATI in her gentle aspect.

SHIVA with the wives of the rishis, whose husbands feared he was trying to seduce them: an episode from the Puranas. *(PAHARI SCHOOL, 1710–25.)*

Her other aspects are called Uma, the gracious; Bhairavi, the terrible; Ambika, the generatrix; Sati, the good wife; Gauri, the brilliant; KALI, the black; and DURGA, the inaccessible.

One myth tells how Shiva gained his third eye as a result of a prank played by Parvati. While Shiva was meditating on Mount Kailasa, Parvati crept up behind him and covered his eyes with her hands. Immediately, the sun grew pale, and every living being trembled with fear. Suddenly, a burning eye appeared on Shiva's forehead, banishing the darkness. Flames shot out from the eye and set light to the whole of the Himalayas. Parvati was devastated and, in due course, Shiva was moved by her distress to restore the mountains to their former glory.

According to another myth, when Shiva was deep in meditation on Mount Kailasa, Parvati grew bored. She persuaded KAMA, god of

SHIVA, as Nataraja, dances holding a drum, symbolizing the rhythm of creation, and a flame, symbolizing destruction.

desire, to come to her aid. Kama was loathe to intervene, but Parvati insisted, whereupon Kama prepared to fire his arrow at Shiva's heart in order to remind him of his duties to his wife. The god Mahesvara saw what was about to happen; since it was necessary for Shiva to finish his meditation in order for the cycles of creation to

run their course, he struck Kama down with a thunderbolt. Later, however, Mahesvara brought Kama back to life.

In another version of the myth, Shiva destroyed Kama with a flash of his third eye. Parvati retired from life, having become tired of Shiva's lack of interest in her. One day she was visited by a young man who, while praising her for her asceticism, tried to persuade her to give it up. Parvati grew angry, and eventually the man revealed himself to be none other than Shiva.

The god promised his wife that he would demonstrate his love to her, but Parvati demanded that he should first return Kama to his wife. Shiva did as she requested, and the couple then retired into the mountains. The intensity of their love-making shook the whole world.

DHYANIBUDDHAS

FIVE GREAT MYSTIC BUDDHAS appear together in the "Mandala of the Five Jinas", and are therefore known collectively as Dhyanibuddhas, or "Meditation Buddhas". They are said to have arisen from the Adibuddha, or "Primeval Buddha". Jinas, or spiritual conquerors, are those who have overcome the perpetual cycle of rebirth and human suffering. As subjects for meditation, they each represent a different aspect of the enlightened consciousness.

Mandala is the Sanskrit word for a circle: a mandala is both a symbolic picture of the universe and an aid to meditation, helping the onlooker to achieve different states of mind. For ritual purposes, the mandala is traced on the ground using coloured powders which are brushed away afterwards. It may also be a picture or a three-dimensional object, such as a sculpture or even a building. Mandalas can also be visualized during meditation – they do not have to exist physically.

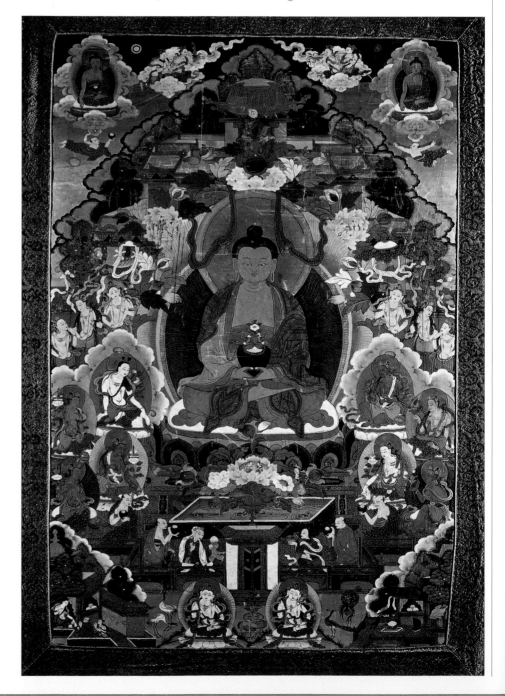

AMITABHA reigns in the western paradise of Sukhavati, or "Pure Land". Once a king, the buddha renounced his throne and vowed to create a realm which combined all the perfections of existing lands. As its ruler, he devoted himself to good deeds and eventually became a buddha. Sitting on his lotus, his aura is bigger than a billion worlds and he has 84,000 marks of his virtues. Rebirth in Pure Land leads to the attainment of nirvana without difficulty. (TIBETAN PAINTING.)

AMOGHASIDDHI (right) rules the paradise of the north, seated on a throne flanked by a pair of garudas, or mythical birds with human heads, on which he travels. He is coloured green, and his hand is traditionally raised in a posture meaning "Fear not". His emblem is the Vajra, the thunderbolt, an indestructible weapon, as hard as a diamond. *(TIBETAN PAINTING, 15TH CENTURY.)*

AKSOBHYA (above), the "Immovable", was a monk who took an oath that he would never again feel anger or revulsion. His adherence to his vow eventually resulted in his attainment of enlightenment. He is the buddha of the eastern paradise, Abhirati, where the virtuous are reborn into a land without evil or suffering and where they can quickly achieve nirvana. He touches the earth with his hand to symbolize his enlightenment. *(LOTUS MANDALA WITH AKSOBHYA, 12TH CENTURY.)*

VAIROCANA (left) is the oldest of the Dhyanibuddhas. His name means "Coming from the Sun", and he was at one time identified with the Adibuddha. He is often depicted clasping his hands in the gesture of supreme wisdom. The great monument of Borobodur, in Java, is itself a mandala, designed in concentric circles and squares with four open entrances. A long series of stone reliefs depicting the Buddha's life story is designed to aid meditation. *(RELIEF OF BUDDHA MAHAVAIROCANA AT BOROBODUR, JAVA, 9TH CENTURY.)*

THE MANDALA (left) has a fixed, symbolic format. It has an outer ring of flames, protecting the area within, and burning away the impurities of the onlooker. A ring of Vajras indicates the indestructability of enlightenment, and lotus petals show the nature of the Pure Land. Within the circles is a palace, with four walls and four open gates, symbolizing the whole world. At the centre sits a presiding deity, with whom the meditator attempts to identify. *(SAMVARA MANDALA, TIBET.)*

SITA (left) and Lakshmana, Rama's half-brother, watch the monkey god Hanuman worshipping Rama.

SITA (right) finds Rama among the lotus blooms. (PAINTING BY WARWICK GOBLE.)

SHRI see LAKSHMI.

SISUPALA see RAVANA.

SITA appears in the Veda, the sacred knowledge of the Hindus, as a goddess who rules over agriculture and vegetation and is the wife of the war god INDRA. However, according to the Hindu epic, the Ramayana, she is the wife of RAMA, an AVATAR of the great god VISHNU, and the daughter of King Janaka.

Rama won Sita as his wife after proving his worth by stringing a miraculous bow, which the god SHIVA had given to the king. RAVANA, the demon king of LANKA, later abducted Sita and took her to his kingdom.

According to one version of the myth, when Rama finally reclaimed his wife, he suspected her of having committed adultery with the demon. Sita proved her innocence and was immediately swallowed by the earth, her mother. Shortly afterwards, Rama drowned. In another version of the traditional tale, Sita demonstrated her innocence by throwing herself on to a funeral pyre, which left her unscathed. The goddess is believed to embody all the virtues of an ideal wife: chaste and devout.

SKANDA see KARTTIKEYA.

SOMA, according to Hindu mythology, is the vital life force in all living beings. A plant, as well as the state of ecstasy induced by the sacred drink extracted from the plant, it played a central role in Vedic sacrificial rituals.

Soma was regarded as a deity, and one entire book of the ten that comprise the Rig Veda, the sacred Hindu hymns, is devoted to his glory. After swallowing the juice, the war god INDRA grew so vast that he filled heaven and earth. It was said to be the power of Soma that enabled Indra to overcome the monstrous snake VRITRA and to make the sun rise. In due course, Soma developed into the moon god. The source of water, he was associated with fertility and the powers of creation.

Sometimes regarded as the father of the gods, Soma was married to the daughters of DAKSHA, a lord of creation. One myth tells how Daksha believed that Soma was showing one of his daughters preference over the others, and so sentenced the moon to death by consumption. However, Daksha's other daughters intervened, causing Soma's punishment to be only periodic rather than eternal. According to another traditional myth, the waxing and waning of the moon is due to the gods'

SITA before Rama – her husband and an incarnation of Vishnu. Lakshmana waves a fan. (ILLUSTRATION BY J. HIGGINBOTHAM, 1864.)

gradual consumption of the Soma it contains. Soma is the equivalent of the ancient Iranian Haoma. Soma can appear as either a bull or a bird.

SUDAPANI see DHANVANTARI.

SUMERU see MERU.

SURABHI see AMRITA.

SURYA, the sun god, was one of the most important deities in the Veda, the sacred knowledge of the Hindus. His father was either the sky god Dyaus or the warrior god INDRA.

Sometimes, however, Surya is said to form a trinity with Indra and the fire god AGNI, who are regarded as his brothers. His mother is ADITI, the mother goddess. According to the Rig Veda, the sacred Hindu hymns, Aditi had eight sons known as the ADITYAS. She threw one of her offspring, the sun, away from her, possibly because she did not want to be associated with its burning heat. Another myth tells how Surya arose from the eye of a great giant, PURUSHA.

Surya has golden hair and golden arms, although sometimes he is represented as dark red in colour. His chariot is drawn by a team of horses and he holds a lotus flower in his hands. His symbol is

the swastika, which was widely used throughout the ancient world as a symbol of the sun.

Surya's scorching heat was so intense that his wife Sanjna became exhausted and left him. Before abandoning the god, she persuaded her handmaid to take her place. Surya went in search of Sanjna and found her in the forest in the form of a mare. The god transformed himself into a horse, and the couple produced the warrior Revanta and the two ASVINS. The Asvins are golden youths who act as messengers of the dawn.

Eventually, Sanjna's father cut off some of Surya's brightness so that Sanjna was able to bear his heat. Surya's shavings fell to earth, where they were made into weapons for the gods.

In the *Brahmapuranas*, sacred writings dating from the fourth century AD, Surya is attributed with 12 "splendours" and given 12 names of distinct deities including INDRA, VISHNU, VARUNA and MITRA. Surya himself is said to be "the supreme spirit who, by means of these splendours, permeates the universe and radiates as far as the secret soul of men."

SURYA (left), the sun god in Hindu mythology. (LIMESTONE VOTIVE IMAGE FROM THE SUN TEMPLE AT KONARAK, ORISSA, 11TH CENTURY.)

SURYA (below), the Hindu sun god, drives his chariot across the sky. (ILLUSTRATION BY J. HIGGINBOTHAM, 1864.)

T

TAKSHAKA, according to Hindu mythology, was king of the *NAGAS*, the semi-divine serpents. He ruled over a glorious city in the under-world. One myth tells how King Parikchit, when out hunting, mis-takenly insulted a hermit who had taken a vow of silence. The hermit's son cursed the king, saying that within a week the snake Takshaka would burn and kill him with his poison. The king decided to pro-tect himself by building a palace on top of a column in the middle of a lake. Takshaka transformed an army of serpents into monks and sent them to the king with gifts. Among the gifts, the king found a strange insect. He was so relieved that Takshaka had spared him that he boasted to his courtiers that, having no fear of death, he dared to put the insect on his neck. Immediately, the insect turned into Takshaka. The serpent bound the king in his massive coils and uttered a tremendous roar, where-upon the king's courtiers burst into tears and fled. Meanwhile,

Takshaka rose high into the air, king Parikchit fell down dead, and his palace burst into flames.

According to another tale, Takshaka coveted some beautiful jewels, which belonged to the queen, wife of King Parikchit's son. The queen decided to give the jew-els to the wife of a tutor and asked Utanka, one of the tutor's stu-dents, to take them to her. On the journey, Utanka stopped to wash. Immediately, a beggar stole the jew-els and ran off with them. Utanka pursued the beggar, but when he finally caught hold of him, the man turned into the serpent Takshaka, slid into a hole in the ground, and hid in his palace.

The god *INDRA* saw Utanka's distress and sent a thunderbolt down to earth. The bolt split the ground open, allowing Utanka to continue pursuing the thief. Beneath the earth, Utanka discov-ered a glorious kingdom filled with beautiful palaces and temples. He chanted a hymn of praise to the nagas, but the snakes remained

unmoved. Utanka then began to praise Indra. Flattered, Indra again offered to help the student, whose horse burst into flames and

engulfed the nagas' kingdom in smoke. Terrified, Takshaka returned the jewels to Utanka. At long last, riding Indra's horse, Utanka arrived at the appointed place to deliver the jewels to his tutor's wife.

TARA is one of Tibetan Buddhism's most popular deities. Her name means both "She Who Delivers" and "Star". She is regarded as an emanation of the *BODHISATTVA AVALOKITESHVARA* and is said to have been born from a lotus floating in one of his tears in order to help him in his work. According to another account, Tara was born in a beam of blue light

TARA (above) as the Green Tara, is regarded as the saviour of Tibet, and holds the blue lotus of compassion in each hand. (MONGOLIA, 19TH CENTURY.)

TARA (left), in her white form, is the symbol of transcendent knowledge.

TARA (right), the patron goddess of Tibet, has 21 forms, including that of the Green Tara, who embodies the feminine aspect of compassion.

which shone from one of Avalokiteshvara's eyes. She embodies the feminine aspect of compassion and incorporates the essence of the goddess. As a result, her name is sometimes applied to other female deities.

The earliest representations of the goddess date from the sixth century AD, when Tara came to be regarded as the *SHAKTI*, or sometimes the wife, of Avalokiteshvara. In Tibet, where her cult spread widely in the 11th century, it was said that the goddess was reincarnated in every virtuous woman. Since then she has been worshipped widely as a personal deity. There are 21 different forms of Tara, each of which has its own colour, posture and attributes, and they all can appear to be either peaceful or wrathful.

The most common forms are Green Tara and White Tara. In Tibet, the White Tara is often said to be a form of the Green Tara. She is believed to be a form of *SARASVATI*, the wife of *BRAHMA*. The Green Tara, said to be the original Tara, holds a blue lotus in each hand to signify her compassion. The consorts of the seventh-century Tibetan king Songtsen Gampo are said to have been embodiments of these two Taras. When red, yellow or blue, Tara is said to be in a menacing mood, whereas when green or white she is said to be gentle and loving. Tibetan Buddhists believe that their ancestors are

Avalokiteshvara in the form of a monkey and Tara (sGrol-ma) in the form of a rock ogress.

TATHAGATAS see *THE DHYANI-BUDDHAS*.

THE TIRTHANKARAS are the ancient "Ford-makers" of Jainism, who taught the Jain doctrine. These leaders, through their own ascetic observances, succeeded in finding a way of escaping the continual round of death and rebirth, and were thus able to show others the path to enlightenment.

According to Jain belief, there are ten regions of the universe, in each of which 24 tirthankaras appear in each of the three ages – past, present and future. Since Jains do not believe in a creator god, their mythology concentrates on the figures of these tirthankaras, who have become objects of worship. Tirthankaras are usually depicted naked, each with his own characteristic colour and posture, but otherwise identical.

In the current age, the first tirthankara was Rishabha, who is usually said to be the founder of Jainism. At his birth, the great warrior god *INDRA* appeared in order to welcome the child into the world. Rishabha taught human beings how to cultivate the land, how to ply different trades and how to execute the arts. He also organized people into three castes. He then left worldly affairs and became a monk. After meditating for six months, Rishabha achieved enlightenment and finally entered nirvana. Twenty-one tirthankaras followed Rishabha, ending with Neminatha, a cousin of *KRISHNA*.

The twenty-third tirthankara, Parshva, appeared 84,000 years after Neminatha's death. Before being born, Parshva lived in heaven as the god Indra. In order to descend to earth, he entered the womb of Queen Vama. As a child, Parshva disdained worldly life and finally withdrew to live in the forest

as a recluse. Eventually, he learned how to achieve liberation from the world and from then onwards he passed on his knowledge to his followers. When he died, at the age of 100, his soul entered nirvana. His death occurred 246 years before the birth of Mahavira, the twenty-fourth Tirthankara.

Mahavira, or the "Great Hero" was also known as Vardhamana. One night, he entered the womb of Devananda, the wife of a brahman. That same night, Devananda saw 14 apparitions, all of favourable omen – an elephant, a bull, a lion, the goddess Shri, or *LAKSHMI*, a garland, the moon, the sun, a standard, a vase, a lake of lotuses, the ocean, a heavenly dwelling, a heap of jewels and a flame.

Devananda's husband was delighted by this omen, as he felt sure it meant that he would father a wise and learned son. However, the

THE TIRTHANKARA Malli, the nineteenth, was a woman according to one Jain tradition. Tirthankaras are portrayed with downcast eyes, to indicate their detachment. (CHAUHAN SCULPTURE, 11TH CENTURY.)

king of the gods decided that he would prefer Trisala, the wife of Siddhartha, a kshatriya (member of the warrior caste) to bear the child, and so the embryo was transferred. Trisala also witnessed 14 splendid apparitions before the birth.

When Mahavira was born, the gods rejoiced and the demons threw gifts. As a youth, Mahavira married Yasoda, but at the age of 30, he gave away his wealth and withdrew from the world. After 12 years of austerity, he achieved enlightenment. When Mahavira died, his soul ascended to nirvana. Jainism still requires its followers to practise austerity for at least 12 years. (See also *TIRTHANKARAS*)

V

TRANSCENDENT BUDDHAS
see *DHYANIBUDDHAS*.

TUSHITA is the Buddhist heaven inhabited by contented or joyful gods. It is home to all the buddhas who need to be born on earth only once more, and is thus the abode of *MAITREYA*, the future buddha. Before his final incarnation, *GAUTAMA BUDDHA* lived in the Tushita heaven as a *BODHISATTVA*. From there, he descended to earth to enter the right side of Queen *MAYA*, his mother. In the Tushita heaven, one day corresponds to 400 years of human life.

UPULVAN is the highest of the four great gods in the Singhalese pantheon. His name means the "Water-lily Coloured One". He is said to have been the only god who remained faithful to *GAUTAMA BUDDHA* during his battle with the demon *MARA*.

URVASI see *APSARAS*.

USHA see *ANIRUDDHA*.

USHAS, the dawn, is the daughter of *PRITHIVI*, the earth goddess of Hindu mythology. Her father is usually said to be the sky god Dyaus and her lover *SURYA*, the sun god. Sometimes, however, the fire god *AGNI* is regarded as her lover, and she herself is said to be the mother of the sun. According to another tradition, Ushas was the daughter of *PRAJAPATI*, the lord or master of created beings. When the god attempted to commit incest with her, Ushas turned into a deer in order to escape his advances.

Ushas is the bringer of life in all its richness. She drives away the dark but is the source of aging. She herself is born each morning, yet because she exists for ever, she is regarded as old. It is said that through the light provided by Ushas, human beings can find their way towards the truth. Each morning, like a good housewife, she wakes all living beings and directs them towards their work. The gods implore her to leave the wicked asleep and wake only the good. In the *Rig Veda*, the ancient sacred hymns, Ushas is depicted as a bride dressed in rose-coloured garments and a golden veil. She is sometimes described as a dancing girl, covered with jewels, or as a beautiful young woman who is stepping out of her bath. The goddess drives a carriage pulled by rosy-hued cows or horses, who represent the morning clouds.

VAIROCANA, according to Hindu mythology, was an *ASURA*, the son of Prahlada, who became king of the *DAITYAS*. He was the father of Bali, who was overcome by *VISHNU* in his incarnation as a dwarf.

One account tells how, together with *INDRA*, Vairocana attempted to discover Atman, or the "Self". The gods sent Indra and Vairocana to ask *PRAJAPATI* to help them in their quest, whereupon Prajapati told them, "That which is reflected in the eye, that is the Self." Vairocana

VAIROCANA is the principal of the five Dhyanibuddhas, or "Great Buddhas of Wisdom". (TIBET, 15TH CENTURY.)

and Indra then asked whether that which was reflected in the water was the Self. Prajapati confirmed their suspicion and told them to look at themselves in the water. He added that they should let him know if there was anything they failed to understand. Vairocana decided that he now knew the Self, and returned to the asuras. Indra looked at himself in the water but was troubled by numerous questions which he put to Prajapati. Eventually, Indra achieved absolute certainty about the Self and became fully enlightened.

Vairocana appears in Buddhist teaching as the principal of the five *DHYANIBUDDHAS*, or the "Great Buddhas of Wisdom". He is said to be the personification of the "Absolute" and is sometimes regarded as a type of *ADIBUDDHA*, or primordial Buddha. In Tibet, the snow lion is regarded as Vairocana's mount. His colour is white, and he is often shown holding a disc. Vairocana is sometimes said to have introduced humankind to the Yogacara school of Mahayana, or "Great Vehicle" Buddhism, which teaches that everything is "mind only" and that the disciple's aim is to achieve mystical union with the divine. (See also *DHYANIBUDDHAS*)

VAISHRAVANA see *GUARDIAN KINGS*.

THE VAJRA, or Vajrakila, is a deified spike, sometimes known as a "Thunderbolt Sceptre", which is believed to embody a powerful god and is said to be capable of dispelling evil forces. It is mainly employed by Tantric Buddhists in Tibet. The Vajra originated in India, where the thunderbolt sceptre is the favourite weapon of *INDRA*.

VAJRAVARAHI is regarded as an important Buddhist deity in both Tibet and Nepal. Her name means "Diamond Sow", and she is represented with the head of a pig. Her attributes are a thunderbolt, a skull and a club.

VAMANA see *AVATARS*.

VARAHA see *AVATARS*.

THE VAJRA, or "Thunderbolt Sceptre", is carried by the god Indra, the Hindu god of weather, mounted on Airavata.

VARUNA appears in the *Rig Veda*, an ancient collection of sacred Hindu hymns, as a sky god. He symbolized the heavens and lived in his palace high above the realm in which *INDRA* operated. In one sense, then, he was more important than Indra, but because he was more remote, the part he played was of less consequence. He could see everything going on in the world and surveyed the affairs of human beings, reading their secret thoughts and sending his messengers out to oversee their activities. Varuna was omnipresent and knew both the past and the future. Above all, he was concerned with the moral order. He presided over oaths and he initiated and sustained the *rta* or order, which was believed to govern both nature and society, and which human beings had to obey. Those who failed to follow the *rta* would be bound with Varuna's noose. However, the god had a reputation for gentleness and could undo sin easily. Varuna was sometimes said to have created the sun; at other times, the sun was said to be his eye. Later, he came to be seen as lord of the night and as the god of water, ruler of the rivers and seas. The wind was his breath,

and the stars his eyes. He was linked with the moon, and presided over the care of *SOMA*, the sacred drink. He also shared with *YAMA*, the first person who died, the title of "King of the Dead". Sometimes regarded as one of the *ADITYAS* and the twin brother of *MITRA*, Varuna is also known as "King of the Snakes".

VASUDEV see *KRISHNA*.

VASUKI see *NAGAS*.

VAYU appears in the *Veda*. He is god of the winds and sometimes shares a chariot with *INDRA*. He is said to have been born from the breath of *PURUSHA*, the original being or world giant.

According to one myth, Vayu was responsible for creating the island of *LANKA*, now known as Sri Lanka. Narada, a sage or *RISHI*, challenged Vayu, who was known for his unstable temper, to break off the summit of Mount *MERU*. *GARUDA*, the mythical bird, protected the mountain, but one day, in the bird's absence, Vayu succeeded in his efforts. He immediately threw the mountain peak into the sea where it became the island of Lanka.

VARUNA (left) was represented riding a sea monster and holding the noose he used to bind the disobedient. (STONE, 8TH CENTURY.)

THE LIFE OF THE BUDDHA

BEFORE HE ACHIEVED enlightenment, the Buddha had lived through a long series of existences as a bodhisattva, striving to be generous and moral, to shun possessions and to gain insight. He was eventually reborn in the Tushita heaven, the domain of those who need be born only once more, where he prepared

for his final miraculous birth as Siddharta Gautama. King Snddhodana, his father, had been told in a prophecy that if his son were to be king, he must be prevented from seeing the miseries of life. So, Siddharta enjoyed a splendid and carefree life in three palaces, surrounded by guards to stop him from looking out. He married Yasodhara and had a son, Rahula. But at about the age of 30, he ventured out of his palaces and encountered the "Four Sights": old age, disease, death and an ascetic looking for a way to transcend suffering. Siddharta resolved to do the same and left his royal existence behind.

QUEEN MAYA (above), the Buddha's mother, dreamed on the night of his conception that an elephant laid a lotus blossom in her womb while the whole of nature shook with joy. At his birth, the Buddha emerged from his mother's side while she rested by a tree in a garden. He began to walk immediately, and lotus flowers sprang up each time his feet touched the ground. With seven symbolic steps, one in each of the cardinal directions, he took possession of the world and declared that there would be no more rebirth for him. (SCENES FROM BUDDHA'S LIFE BY MULGANDHA VIGARA.)

GAUTAMA BUDDHA (left), having left behind his early life of absolute luxury, endured six years of strict austerities which reduced him to little more than a skeleton. Eventually, however, he realized that this way of life would do nothing to end human suffering and that he needed to achieve a middle way. On the bank of the river Nairanjana, a woman called Sujata mistook him for a god and made him an offering of rice milk, which he accepted. Knowing now that his enlightenment was near, he divided the milk into 49 mouthfuls, one for each day he would spend in contemplation, striving to see things as they really are. (FROM A PAINTING BY ABANINDRO NATH TAGORE.)

GAUTAMA BUDDHA (left) spent the 45 years following his enlightenment wandering and preaching the truths he had learnt. He taught everywhere he went, talking to everyone from kings to beggars, and lived by begging himself. He converted all those he met and performed many miracles, and his following increased in number. A community of Buddhist monks, the Sangha, grew up. (THE BUDDHA BEING OFFERED HERBS, TIBETAN, 18TH CENTURY.)

ANANDA (below), the Buddha's first cousin and devoted attendant, was one of his disciples who attained enlightenment in his presence. Ananda recited the Buddha's teachings at the first Buddhist council. He could explain all 60,000 words and was known as the "Treasurer of the Teachings". He was also responsible for encouraging women to join the Sangha, and established an order of nuns. (BURMESE SHRINE.)

GAUTAMA BUDDHA (above) sat under the Bodhi tree in Bodh Gaya for 49 days, and achieved enlightenment when his knowledge was crystallized into the "Four Noble Truths": that life is full of suffering, that suffering depends on craving, that suffering can be ended, that the way to end it is to follow the eightfold path: right view, right thought, right speech, right action, right livelihood, right effort, right mindfulness and right concentration. His initial response was to remain where he was, but he was persuaded by the god Brahma to preach the truth he had discovered to his growing band of disciples.

THE VIDYARAJAS are Buddhism's semi-divine kings of mystical knowledge. They symbolize the power which the five *DHYANIBUDDHAS*, "Great Buddhas of Wisdom", exert over the passions and forces of evil. They are sometimes regarded as wrathful emanations of the Dhyanibuddhas, or as the energy which the adept assumes on meeting obstacles.

In India and the Hindu pantheon, the Vidyarajas are represented by the Bhairavas, the "Terrifying Ones", and the Krodharajas, or "Kings of Wrath", who eat flesh. The five great Vidyarajas correspond to the five Dhyanibuddhas, while other Vidyarajas correspond to the *BODHISATTVAS*. Acalanatha corresponds to the Dhyanibuddha *VAIROCANA*, Trailokyavijaya corresponds to *AKSOBHYA*, Kundali corresponds to *RATNASAMBHAVA*, *YAMANTAKA* corresponds to *AMITABHA*, and Vajrayaksa or Vajrapani corresponds to *AMOGHASIDDHI*.

VINATA see *GARUDA*.

VISHNU is one of the most important gods of Hinduism and the most widely worshipped. Together with *SHIVA* and *BRAHMA*, he belongs to the triad of great gods known as the Trimurti. The preserver of the world, Vishnu is majestic and at times terrifying. On the whole, however, he is a benevolent deity and far less frightening than Shiva. Vishnu's devotees, the Vaishnavas, regard him as the supreme god: one of his many epithets is the "Highest God". Brahman, the Hindu concept of the "Absolute" or supreme reality, is sometimes depicted as Vishnu.

According to one myth, a lotus flower emerged from Vishnu's navel on the end of a long stalk held by *VAYU*, the vital force and god of the winds. Seated in the centre of the flower was Brahma, who subsequently proceeded with the act of creation.

VISHNU sits enthroned on the coils of the world snake Ananta or Sesha, on which he sleeps during the intervals between Brahma's successive creations. He holds a shell, mace, disc and lotus.
(*IVORY STATUETTE.*)

Vishnu's main function is to ensure the triumph of good over evil. In the *Rig Veda*, the ancient sacred hymns of Hinduism, Vishnu appears as only a minor deity. He seems to have originated as a solar god, and in his manifestation as the sun, he was said to be able to traverse the cosmos in only three steps, an act probably intended to symbolize the god measuring out the universe, making it habitable for gods and humans. Later, Vishnu began to be associated with other figures, including a fish and a dwarf. This association developed into the concept of Vishnu's incarnations, known as *AVATARS*, or "descents". Vishnu appears in these different guises in order to combat demons and to restore divine order when the cosmos is threatened. The most important of Vishnu's avatars are the hero, *RAMA*, and the god, *KRISHNA*. Within Hinduism, *GAUTAMA BUDDHA* also came to be regarded as one of the great god's incarnations.

In his incarnation as the fish Matsya, Vishnu saved *MANU*, the first man, from a great flood. The tale tells how Manu found a tiny fish, which begged him to rescue it from the other fish, which were trying to eat it. Manu took the fish home and kept it in a pot. Soon the fish grew too big for the pot, so Manu put it into a pond. Matsya then grew too big for the pond, so Manu took it to the ocean.

As Manu released the fish into the waters, Matsya turned and warned him that there was to be a great flood, which would drown the whole world. He advised Manu to save himself by building a boat. The floods arrived and Manu took shelter in his boat. Fierce waves and winds attacked the boat, and Matsya again appeared, this time as a gigantic fish. Matsya towed the boat behind him for several years until he reached Mount Hemavat, the summit of which remained above the waters. Manu moored the boat to the mountain and awaited the end of the flood. Matsya then announced that he was in fact Vishnu and that he had saved Manu so that he could repopulate the world.

In his incarnation as the dwarf Vamana, Vishnu saved the world from the demon Bali. He persuaded Bali to give him as much land as he could cover in three strides. As soon as Bali granted his request, Vishnu was transformed into a giant. In two strides, he crossed the universe, which he returned to the gods. He then turned to the demon and insisted that he be allowed to take a third step, as promised. Bali offered Vishnu his head to stand upon and, in recognition of this honourable behaviour, Vishnu gave the demon the underworld to rule as his kingdom.

In the intervals between Brahma's successive creations, Vishnu is believed to lie asleep on the cosmic waters, on top of the many-headed world snake Ananta or Sesha. During his sleep, he slowly develops into another avatar, who will appear in the impending cycle of creation.

Vishnu is usually depicted as a beautiful young man, blue in colour and with four arms. His attributes include the club, associated with the power of knowledge; a conch shell, associated with the origins of existence; a wheel, associated with the powers of creation and destruction; and the lotus, which is associated with the sun and with the tree of life that springs from Vishnu's navel. His mount is the mythical bird GARUDA.

The god is also identified with the cosmic pillar, the centre of the universe which was believed to support the heavens. His consort is LAKSHMI, the goddess of wealth and good fortune. (See also THE AVATARS OF VISHNU)

VISHVAKARMA see LANKA.

VIVASVAT see YAMA.

VRINDA see ASURAS.

VRITRA was the fearsome serpent of Hindu mythology whom the great god INDRA destroyed. He embodied the dark and unproductive forces of nature, and deprived humanity of the light of knowledge. A powerful Brahman called Tvashtri was determined to overthrow Indra. He fathered a son, Trisiras, whom he strengthened with his own powers. The son had three heads; he read the Veda with

VISHNU, the supreme cosmic principle, forms a triad of great gods with Brahma and Shiva. (STONE, 10TH CENTURY.)

VISHNU, attended by his consort, Lakshmi, sleeps on the world snake, Sesha, while Brahma, the creator, emerges from the lotus growing from Vishnu's navel. (MINIATURE, RAJASTHAN, 18TH CENTURY.)

his first head, he fed himself with the second head and he used his third head for surveying the world. He was exceedingly pious, and Indra became worried as his power seemed to increase day after day. Indra sent beautiful young women to seduce Trisiras, but nothing tempted him from his path of asceticism. Eventually, Indra decided to kill him and struck him down with his thunderbolt. However, even then the boy continued to radiate such a splendid light over the entire world that Indra's fears were unallayed.

Tvashtri, the boy's father, determined to avenge the death of his son and created a huge and terrifying demon called Vritra. The demon challenged Indra to a battle, and a bloody and terrifying onslaught ensued. Eventually,

Vritra swallowed the god. The assembly of deities was horrified and decided to make the demon open his mouth. As soon as Vritra did so, Indra jumped out, and the battle began again.

Eventually, a great RISHI, or sage, was consulted and, with the help of VISHNU, a truce was agreed upon. Vritra promised to make peace, provided that Indra never attacked him with a weapon of wood, stone or iron, nor with anything wet or dry, nor during the night or day. Indra agreed, but he continued to plot his revenge on the demon.

At sunset one evening he saw a pillar of foam, neither wet nor dry nor wood, stone, nor iron, arising from the sea. He took the pillar and threw it at Vritra, who immediately fell dead. After slaying the demon, Indra liberated the waters, the sun, the sky and the dawn.

Y

THE YAKSHAS, according to Hindu mythology, are followers of the god of riches, Kuvera. They live in the Himalayas and guard hidden treasure. The yakshas are usually depicted with short limbs and pot bellies. They are often benign, and are worshipped as protective spirits and bringers of fertility. Female yakshas are known as yakshis. In Buddhism, the yakshas are sometimes wild creatures who haunt lonely places and show hostility towards people by disturbing their meditations.

In Tibet, the yakshas are known as gnod-sbyin. Regarded as semidivine beings, they resemble nature

YAKSHAS (left) are Hindu nature spirits. The female spirits, yakshis, though graceful, can be spiteful and sometimes eat children. (SANDSTONE BRACKET, 2ND CENTURY AD.)

spirits and protect Buddha and the Buddhist law. According to one tradition, Tibet was originally ruled over by a succession of beings, the first of whom were the black and warlike gnod-sbyin.

YAMA appears in the *Rig Veda*, the ancient sacred hymns of Hinduism. He is the guardian of hell and is regarded as "King of the Dead". A fierce deity, he is usually said to be the son of Vivasvat, the sun, and the brother of MANU, the only survivor of the great flood. Yama's companion and sister was Yamuna, or Yami.

The brother and sister are sometimes said to have been the first human couple, and Yama to have been the first man who died. According to one story, Yama set out to explore the world and discovered a path to heaven. As a result, mortality was introduced to the world. As the guardian of the dead, Yama was originally regarded as a friendly deity. However, by the time of the *Brahmanas*, the Hindu texts, which were commentaries on the Veda, or "Sacred Knowledge", Yama had become a sinister and destructive force. He developed into the terrifying punisher of human beings, and was depicted armed with a noose and a mace, green in colour, and with two four-eyed dogs as companions. These dogs would sometimes wander the world, gathering together the souls of the dying.

When the soul leaves the body, it is said to cross the river Vaitarani to the land of the dead, where it proceeds towards the judgment room. There, an account of the

YAMA (right) with Naciketas, a man to whom Yama taught the secret of immortality. Yama is regarded as the guardian of hell and "King of the Dead".

soul's deeds is read out, whereupon Yama makes his judgment. The soul will be sent either to a paradise, to one of many hells, or back to the world of the living, where it will be reborn.

One myth tells how the devoted Savitri persuaded Yama to give her back her husband Satyavan. Yama, impressed by her love, offered to grant her a wish as long as she did not ask him to restore Satyavan to life. She agreed, but wished for more sons fathered by her husband, so Yama had to send him back to keep his promise.

In Buddhist mythology, Yama is the ruler of the hells. Originally he was a king of Vaishali, a city in north-eastern India. During a ferocious battle, the king wished that he was the ruler of hell and was reborn as Yama. He was accompanied to hell by his eight generals and 80,000 soldiers. There, he has molten copper poured into his mouth three times a day. The punishment will last until all Yama's deeds have been atoned for. In the meantime, he inflicts disease and old age on humans, to prevent them from living immoral lives.

Yama's sister, Yami, is said to rule over the females in hell. In Tibetan Buddhism, Yama is often shown accompanied by Yami and is sometimes regarded as one of the DHARMAPALAS, or "Protectors of the Teaching".

YAMA with his shakti, Yami, goddess of death. They stand in the posture of Yab-Yum on Yama's attendant animal, a black buffalo. Yama is a guardian of the south, the direction associated with the dead.

YAMANTAKA, or "He Who Puts an End to Yama", is one of Buddhism's *VIDYARAJAS*, or kings of mystical knowledge. He conquers *YAMA*, god of the dead, and is sometimes shown trampling him. A wrathful manifestation of the buddha *AKSOBHYA*, he is one of the *BODHISATTVAS* who welcome the faithful into Aksobhya's paradise. He is also regarded as a *DHARMAPALA*, or "Protector of the Teaching", and is said to fight pain.

Yamantaka is often shown with six arms and legs as well as six horribly contorted faces, each with three eyes. He is usually represented seated on a white cow, although he sometimes rests on a rock. His body is coloured black, dark blue or green, and he is surrounded by flames. In Tibet, he is sometimes shown holding an axe and a skull, and he may wear a tiara of skulls, a belt of skulls and carry a human corpse.

YAMI; YAMUNA see *YAMA*.

YASHODA see *KRISHNA*.

THE YIDAMS are the tutelary deities of Tibet. There are numerous yidams since each deity in the Tibetan pantheon can be adopted

YAMANTAKA is a wrathful guardian deity of Tibetan Buddhism, depicted in the posture of embrace, or Yab-Yum, with his shakti, Vidyadhara.

as a tutelary god. Their name means "Firm Mind". The yidams are invoked by people for protection, but they are more usually regarded as deities who can help in an individual's transformation. They are nearly always depicted with their *SHAKTI*, their corresponding female energies, and are usually coloured blue. The male yidams are divided into bhagavats, dakas and herukas, whereas the female yidams are divided into bhagavatis and *DAKINIS*.

THE YUGAS are Hinduism's cycles, or ages of the world. Each yuga lasts for thousands, even millions, of years.

The yugas decline in length through the cycle, reflecting the decline in righteousness. The Krita Yuga, lasting 1,728,000 human years, was the golden age, when there were no gods, demons or diseases and when human beings were saints. The Treta Yuga lasted 1,296,000 years and was the age when sacrifices began and people became less virtuous. The Dwapara Yuga was a decadent age, lasting 864,000 years, when virtue lessened even more and desire, disease and disasters entered the world. The Kali Yuga, 432,000 years long, is the degenerate age, when only a quarter of virtue remains and people have sunk into wickedness. The Kali Yuga is the age in which we are currently living.

More than four million human years make up a Maha Yuga, or great age, and one Maha Yuga equals a day and a night in the life of Brahma. Each Maha Yuga is preceded and followed by periods of twilight, which last a tenth of the length of a Maha Yuga. During this time, *BRAHMA* sleeps.

ZHANG ZHUNG see *GSHEN-RAB*.

FAMILY TREES

SHIVA'S FAMILY

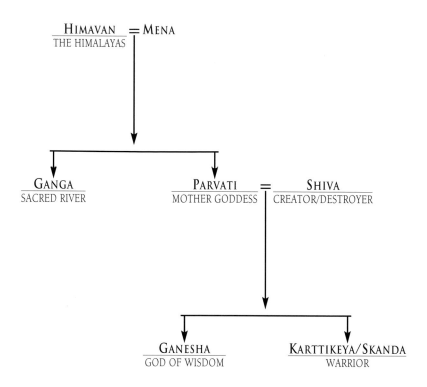

HIMAVAN = MENA
THE HIMALAYAS

GANGA
SACRED RIVER

PARVATI = SHIVA
MOTHER GODDESS | CREATOR/DESTROYER

GANESHA
GOD OF WISDOM

KARTTIKEYA/SKANDA
WARRIOR

Shiva is both the creator and the destroyer, and Parvati is the gentle aspect of his shakti, or creative energy. She is also an aspect of the great goddess, Devi, and a reincarnation of Shiva's wife Sati, who committed suicide. In her subservience to her husband, Parvati is a model for mortal devotees of Shiva.

SHIVA as Nataraja, "Lord of the Dance".

VEDIC CREATION MYTH

DYAUS = ADITI
CREATOR | MOTHER

VIVASVAT/SURYA = SANJNA
SUN GOD | CONSCIENCE

REVANTA
PROTECTOR OF HUNTERS

YAMA
RULERS OF THE UNDERWORLD

YAMI
RULERS OF THE UNDERWORLD

MANU = IDA

HUMANITY

The Vedic religion acknowledged that the origin of the universe is a mystery, and offered many differing accounts of the creation. The lineage of humanity, represented by Manu, the first man, is sometimes traced back through the sun god, the source of heat and life on earth, to the mother of the gods, Aditi.

HIERARCHY OF VEDIC DEITIES

HEAVEN

DYAUS	VARUNA	MITRA	PUSAN	VISHNU
SKY	RIGHTEOUSNESS	LIGHT	NOURISHER	CREATOR

ATMOSPHERE

INDRA	VAYU	RUDRA	THE MARUTS
RAIN	WIND	DESTRUCTION	STORM

EARTH

SOMA	AGNI	BRHASPATI
PLANTS	FIRE	PRIEST, LORD OF PRAYER

The ancient heavenly deities: Dyaus, Varuna, Mitra, Pusan and Vishnu, were endowed with universal power, but were remote figures to most mortals. In contrast Indra and the other gods of the atmosphere, (Vayu, Rudra and the Maruts) exert a more direct influence over human life. Agni is the god of the sacrificial fire, and is therefore an intercessor between the gods and humankind and much closer and less remote than any of the other gods.

THE AVATARS surround this picture of the god Vishnu. The avatars are his incarnations on earth in order to help humankind in moments of great crisis. It is generally accepted that Vishnu has ten avatars, although their number varies and their identities are also flexible. Usually the avatars are said to consist of Matsya, Kurma, Varaha, Narasimha, Vamana, Parashurama, Rama, Krishna, Gautama Buddha and Kalkin.

CHRONOLOGY

c 3200 BC	Rise of the Indus Valley civilization along the banks of the Indus River, with two principal cities: the first, Harappa in the north and the second, Mohenjo-Daro, 350 miles to the south. Examples of a written language have been found but not deciphered.
3102 BC	Beginning of the Hindu Kali Yuga, the present age, due to last 432,000 years.
Before 3000 BC	Evidence of earliest settlements in India: isolated villages with distinct cultures.
2500-2000 BC	Evidence of trade and cultural links between the Indus Valley civilization and the inhabitants of Mesopotamia.
c 1600 BC	Collapse of the Indus Valley civilization, possibly due to an alteration in the course of the river caused by a natural disaster. Written language disappears.
1600-1000 BC	Early Vedic period
c 1500 BC	First wave of Aryan immigration from Central Asia into Indus Valley region.

14th-10th centuries BC	Composition of the Rig Veda, a collection of Sanskrit hymns at first only preserved orally.
1000-600 BC	Late Vedic period
c 1000 BC	Caste system begins to emerge.
c 900 BC	Mahabharata war.
9th century BC	Birth of Parshva, son of Queen Vama of Benares, the 23rd Jain tirthankara.
c 800 BC	Rise of the Brahmans, or priestly caste.
8th-5th centuries BC	Composition of the Upanishads. The Hindu doctrine of rebirth emerges.
6th century BC	Indian voyages to Burma and the Malay Peninsula in search of gold and tin.
566 or 563 BC	Birth of Siddhartha Gautama, founder of Buddhism, in Kapilavastu in the Himalayas.
549 BC	Birth of Mahavira, founder of Jainism, and the 24th tirthankara.
537 BC	The Persian empire of Cyrus II extends to the west of the Indus River.
c 523 BC	Enlightenment of Gautama Buddha occurs at Bodh Gaya.
517-509 BC	The Indus Valley region is conquered by the Persians under Darius.
5th century BC	Rise of the Magadha Empire.
5th-2nd centuries BC	Composition of the Mahabharata, including the Bhagavad Gita.
c 486 BC	Death of Gautama Buddha. First Buddhist council assembles at Rajagriha to compile doctrine and the monastic code.
c 400 BC	The Sutra of Panini, the first Sanskrit grammar, is written.
4th century BC	Earliest evidence of written language since loss of Indus Valley script.
386-376 BC	Second Buddhist Council is held at Vaisali, north of the Ganges.

326 BC	Alexander the Great reaches India in his conquest of the Persian empire.
323 BC	Death of Alexander the Great at Babylon.
322-185 BC	Mauryan Empire
322 BC	Accession of Chandragupta, founder of the Mauryan dynasty. The capital is established at Pataliputra (Patna).
304 BC	Chandragupta Maurya acquires control of the Indus Valley region, presenting Seleucus, Alexander's heir, with 500 elephants in exchange.
3rd century BC	Mahinda introduces Buddhism to Sri Lanka.
273-232 BC	Reign of Ashoka, who, as a Buddhist, issues moral edicts (carved in stone) in line with his beliefs. The Mauryan Empire reaches the height of its power, and controls most of India.
251-246 BC	Sri Lanka is occupied by Aryans.
247 BC	The Third Buddhist Council is held at Pataliputra to compile the canon of Buddhist scriptures. It results in a schism which in due course leads to the development of what is known as Mahayana or "Great Vehicle" Buddhism.
c 200 BC	Bactrian Greeks invade Gandhara.

c 200 BC-AD 800	Creation of rock-hewn Buddhist and Jain monastic chambers and shrines at Ajanta in Deccan, and other sites.
184 BC	The last king of the Mauryan dynasty is assassinated. Rise of the Shunga dynasty.
115-90 BC	Reign of Menander, Bactrian Greek ruler of northwest India.
c 50 BC	Beginning of Shaka era.
c 50 AD	Invasion of Kushans from Mongolia. Trade routes open up between Asia and the Mediterranean. A Zoroastrian temple is built in the Kushan city of Sirsukh (Taxila).
1st/2nd centuries	Height of Brahma's cult.
320-540	Gupta dynasty
385-414	Reign of Chandra Gupta II, who establishes his capital at Ayodhya.
405-411	The Chinese pilgrim Fa Xian travels through India.
5th century	Composition of the Puranas and Ramayana.
510	First recorded act of suttee.
605-647	Reign of Harsha Vardhana of Kanauj.
620-649	Reign of King Songsten Gampo, who invites missionaries from India and China to introduce Buddhism to Tibet.
630-645	The Chinese scholar Xuan Zang travels widely through India.
8th century	Padmasambhava, the "second Buddha", founds Lamaism in Tibet.
712	Arab conquest of Sind.
755-797	Reign of King Trisong Detsen of Tibet.
788	Birth of the philosopher Shankara, who regenerates Hindu orthodoxy.
9th-13th centuries	Chola Empire.
937	Zoroastrians flee Arab oppression in Persia and found the Parsi community in Gujerat.

985-1014	Reign of Rajaraja I, who expands the empire and institutes local self-government.
10th century	South Indian craftsmen perfect their metalworking technique in bronze sculptures of Nataraja, the dancing Shiva.
10th-11th centuries	Development of Sufism.
11th century	Rise of the concept of the Adibuddha.
11th century	Rise of cult of Tara in Tibet.
c 1020-1030	Sultan Mahmud of Ghazni, the "idol-breaker", invades northern India 17 times, massacring Hindus and looting and destroying temples, including the great temple of Somnath.
12th century	Buddhism becomes dominant faith of Tibet.
1206	Genghis Khan conquers Tibet and it remains under Mongol rule until 1720.
1206-1290	Slave dynasty
1206	Following Afghan conquest, Kurb-ud-din becomes sultan of Muslim northern India, of which Delhi becomes the capital.
1221	Mongol invasion of India under Genghis Khan.
1288 and 1293	Marco Polo visits India from the Chinese court of Kublai Khan.
1398	Mongol army led by Timur invades India and sacks Delhi.
15th century	Persian replaces Sanskrit as the official language of northern India and regional languages such as Bengali and Hindi arise.
1469	Birth of Guru Nanak, founder of Sikhism.
1498	First voyage of Vasco da Gama, opening the era of European expansion in South Asia.
1510	Goa captured by the Portuguese.
1526-1707	Moghul Empire
1526	Babur declares himself sultan at Agra and Delhi, instituting Moghul dynasty.

1556-1605	Reign of Akbar, who expands the Moghul Empire to cover the whole of northern India. The Grand Trunk Road is constructed, running from Kabul to Calcutta.
1560	Inquisition established in Goa.
1599	Formation of the East India Company.
17th century	Mahakala, or Mgon-po, adopted as tutelary god of Mongolia.
1627-1658	Reign of Shah Jahan.
1632-1648	Building of the Taj Mahal.
1720	Chinese Qing dynasty claims sovereignty over Tibet.
1757	Battle of Plassey leads to British rule in India.
1768	Nepal is united under Gurkha rule.
1912	Tibetans assert independence from China.
1922	Excavation begins at two main sites in the Indus Valley, Harappa and Mohenjo-Dara, finding evidence of sophisticated brick buildings, street plans and plumbing systems.
1947	Indian independence and creation of Pakistan.
1965	China annexes Tibet and suppresses Tibetan religion, culture and language.

INDEX

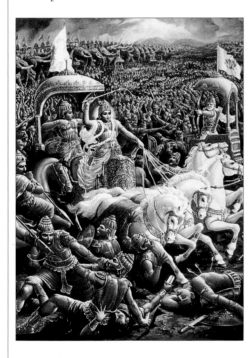

The Publishers are grateful to the agencies listed below for kind permission to reproduce the following images in this book.

AKG, London: p6 SMPK, Berlin; p9tr; p12t Sammlung G.W. Essen, Hamburg; p14l private collection; p15r State Hermitage, St Petersburg; p30t J. Speelman Ltd, London; p30b State Hermitage, St Petersburg; p31tl; p31tr State Hermitage, St Petersburg; p31br; p33t Musee Guimet, Paris; p36t; p42t; p43t Lucknow Museum; p43b; p45b Rose Art Museum, Waltham, Mass,; p51; p65br SMPK, Berlin; p69t State Hermitage, St Petersburg; p75tl Musee Guimet, Paris; p78t Fine Arts Museum, Ulan Bator; p80 State Hermitage, St Petersburg; p85b. Ancient Art and Architecture: p9tl; p20t; p22t; p25t; p27tl; p37; p41tl; p45t; p53br; p55t; p59tl; p75br; p75tr; p81b; p85t; p87b.Bridgeman Art Library: p13b Victoria & Albert Museum, London; p16 Musee Guimet, Paris; p23 Victoria & Albert Museum, London; p26 private collection; p33br Ashmolean Museum, Oxford; p35t National Museum of India, New Delhi; p36br National Museum of India, New Delhi; p38t Christie's; p47t National Museum of India, New Delhi; p48t British Library, London; p48br National Museum of India, New Delhi; p49tr National Museum of India, New Delhi; p49br Dinodia Picture Agency, Bombay; p52t National Museum of India, New Delhi; p53t private collection; p62t Oriental Museum, Durham University; p63 Victoria & Albert Museum, London; p64t Fitzwilliam Museum, University of Cambridge; p68tl National Museum of India, New Delhi; p68tr National Museum of India, New Delhi; p71t British Library, London; p72t Victoria & Albert Museum, London; p72b Victoria & Albert Museum, London; p73b National Museum of India, New Delhi; p76tl Victoria & Albert Museum, London; p77bl National Museum of India, New Delhi; p84 Freud Museum, London. Christie's Art Gallery: p21tr; p34; p40t; p41tr; p10 and 49mt; p49bl; 66bl; p67t; p67bl; p70t. Corbis: p13tl Historical Picture Agency; p17b Nik Wheeler; p21tl Luca I. Tettoni; p25b Gian Berto Vanni; p57 Luca I. Tettoni; p58t Angelo Hornak; p66br Luca I. Tettoni; p75bl Charles & Josette Lenars; p79t Angelo Hornak; p81t Historical Picture Agency; p83br Luca I. Tettoni; CM Dixon: p13tr; p20b; p33bl; p86t. Edimedia: p24t; p44. ET Archive: p8 Musee Guimet, Paris; p12b Victoria & Albert Museum, London; p14r Musee Guimet, Paris; p19tr Victoria & Albert Museum, London; p21b Victoria & Albert Museum, London; p24b British Library, London; p39 Musee Guimet, Paris; p46t Victoria & Albert Museum, London; p50t British Library, London; p54 Musee Guimet, Paris; p56t Musee Guimet, Paris; p56b Musee Guimet, Paris; p61b Lucien Biton Collection, Paris; p65t Victoria & Albert Museum, London; p83t Musee Guimet, Paris.Mary Evans: p40b. Michael Holford: p31bl; p74.Hutchison Library: P58b J Horner; p59b Gail Goodger. Image Solutions: P60t, p60b; p61tl; p82t. Images of India: P70b. Royal Asiatic Society, London: P29b; p29t.